True History Honoring Faith, Strength, and Courage of Oppressed People

Author: Arnold E. Brooks

Section One
American History, Ancient History, and Politics

Section Two
Highlighting Distortions, Deceptions, and Disunity in America

True History Honoring Faith, Strength, and Courage of Oppressed
People
Copyright © 2010
Arnold E. Brooks

All rights reserved. No part of this book may be reproduced in
any form, except for the inclusion of brief quotations in a review,
without permission in writing from the author or publisher.

Library of Congress Control Number: 2012916992

Contact information:
Arnold Brooks
P.O. Box 1475
Owings Mills, MD 21117-1403

ISBN: 978-0-9771554-1-5

Cover Design © Morris Publishing

Printed in the United States by Morris Publishing®
3212 East Highway 30
Kearney, NE 68847
1-800-650-7888

This book challenges the conception of what is taught and not taught about American History in schools. It also challenges the reader's conception of their knowledge and thinking about what is learned, heard, or read pertaining to slavery, segregation, and integration. It presents a different view of American History and tries to display the human conception about African Americans forced to live in a slave society. This book also highlights the struggle, courage, and strength of Black Americans' fight to survive slavery and segregation. It displays how the will of people to survive by working together in unity for equality and justice for all Americans is a significant goal.

African Americans still have a battle to fight and it includes the struggle to protect their victories from the civil rights era. Blacks have knocked down barriers of the past that have denied them freedom, and are a people that will not hesitate to challenge injustice in America.

Our departed leader, Dr. Martin Luther King Jr., said, "Injustice anywhere is Injustice everywhere."

Table of Contents

Chapters

Introduction

Introduction

This book was written in honor of and respect for my race and ancestors who suffered under the inhuman system of slavery in America. It was also written in honor of and respect for those liberal Whites who have died for the freedom of Blacks in their struggles against slavery, racism, and segregation.

I was born in the year 1926 and raised in America during the Thirties and Forties. Being a Black man of African descent, I thank my creator I was not born in America during the era of Slavery. America was a violent, terrorist country for any dark-skinned Americans in the earlier years. The laws were written to protect only White Americans and dehumanize African Americans and Native Americans (formerly known as Indians). Many of the writers of the United States Constitution were slave owners who avidly supported the institution of slavery.

I grew up in America and was educated in American schools. I was taught that America was a country founded on principles of freedom and equality for all human beings. As a child, I was contented and felt proud of my country because of the teachings I received about the greater freedom and opportunities in America compared to those for people living in other countries. The schools, movies, and media bombarded Americans constantly, stating how fortunate they were to live in a free and equal society.

I was raised by a loving mother and father with two older brothers. My mother and father both had jobs and worked all their lives to raise my brothers and me. As I grew older and became a teenager, I remember my mother, father, uncles, aunts, and grandparents talking about the segregated South. I frequently read news articles about racist White mobs lynching Blacks and not being brought to justice for their crimes of mass murder against Black Citizens. When I traveled through the South as a youngster, I encountered firsthand the segregation that was the law there. African Americans were forced to sit in the back of all public transportation. They could not enter many commercial buildings through the front doors; they were forced to enter through the back doors. Blacks could not try on shoes or clothing in clothing stores. Bathrooms and drinking fountains were labeled "White" and "Colored." There were laws to keep the races separated, not permitting them to have open communication or be on any kind of equal footing with each other. All the White accommodations were in tiptop shape and kept clean. All the Black accommodations were poorly kept and poorly cleaned.

As I observed these segregated conditions, I thought about the preaching and teaching in schools, movies, media, and American history books about this being a country of freedom and equality for all of its citizens. I kept wondering how these unjust and unequal conditions could continue to exist within a society that taught and preached that America was a free society which believed in equality. I have lived a good and decent life here in America and received a decent education. I have increased my knowledge of American history by being inquisitive and searching out history books written by a variety of historians. I have asked myself, "How is it possible for a country to preach freedom for all citizens regardless of race or color when it has committed the crimes of race slavery, segregation, etc., and not living up to its rhetoric?" I came to the conclusion that those unjust deeds were not accepted personally by some individuals as long as they were not directly affected by them.

There have been a lot of improvements since my teenage years. Racism is no longer displayed out front, as it had been in the past. Racism was forced to retreat underground, and such practices as lynching are no longer tolerated. There is still the problem of unjust laws and Blacks unfairly and disproportionately sent to prison, etc. This is the reason I have written two books to expose the racist problems in America. This is my second book. My first book is titled, "SSID----- Slavery,Segregation,Integration,Degradation."

I never thought I would live to witness the day when America would try to live up to its rhetoric of being a society of freedom and equality for all. The old racist and segregated days of the past have changed for the better because of the civil rights movements brought about by African Americans and liberal Whites who joined together to tear down the wall of injustice in this country. The election to the presidency of a mixed-race gentleman with African features named Barack Obama proves the majority of Americans are tired of the lies and untruths that have divided them against each other. I will elaborate more on this subject in the two sections of this book.

I was born in South Carolina and my parents moved to Jamaica, Queens, New York when I was an infant. In 1944, I enlisted in the United States Army during the Second World War. After serving in France and Okinawa, I was honorably discharged in 1946. Returning to civilian life after the war; I worked as an orderly attendant at Queens General Hospital in Jamaica, New York. I left that job for employment with the New York City Transit System with the title of Railroad Clerk. My next job was with the New York City Police Department as a Patrolman from 1955 until my retirement in 1976.

After retiring, I returned to work for a short time at a bank in New York City as a mail clerk. An opportunity arose for a new job, which I accepted, with an insurance brokerage firm. I worked at that job as assistant manager of the mail department. After ten years with that firm, I "retired" again. My wife, Estherlene, a native New Yorker, and I lived and enjoyed many happy years in our home in Cambria Heights, New York. In 1994, we decided to relocate to Maryland.

It was during my tour of duty with the N.Y. C. Police Department I became very much interested in history, so I joined a history book club. I have read and collected vast amounts of books about American History and related socio-political subjects. Most of my collection has been donated to Morris College, a Black institution in Sumter, South Carolina. Extensive research on history-specific scholars and biographies of people reporting their personal experiences helped me to discover true American History.

I came to the realization that much of Black History is not taught in American schools. I hoped this would change some day, and that American History would give honor and recognition to all Americans who have made this a strong and prosperous country. I realized that this would not happen under the present conditions and wondered, "What can I do to make a difference?"

My answer was to put African Americans' contributions which made America great into written historical context. I knew this would be quite a task, as it would represent a new way of thinking after centuries of brainwashing used on Black and White citizens. I believe I owe this effort to my ancestors in order to bring honor and respect to their survival after living under horrendous conditions. The holocaust of torture, rape, and murder that they endured, along with the sacrifices they made to protect their children, is something that made me proud to call them my ancestors. I hope this book will pay honor and give them the respect that is due them from their descendants, including all future generations to come.

Throughout history, words, events, religions, etc., have been interpreted to benefit the interests of nations, governments, or races. That is the way the world operates because humans comprise a vain species with different egos. Some government officials, people in power, or politicians trying to influence or persuade people into their way of thinking have used word interpretations with a biased approach to convince people to agree with them.

I hope that this book will help people to unify a little more and be more understanding and tolerant of human differences. Most humans want and need the same substance for survival which is cooperation and peace with each other. African Americans are proud to admit their ancestors are from the great Black race of Africa, the cradle of civilization, and have accepted America as their home and country that they will defend against its enemies.

Political parties are not highlighted extensively in this book as much as the problem of racism is presented. There are three main political parties in America. Their names are Republican, Democratic, and Independent. I have not specifically mentioned what these parties stand for; I have discussed specific groups such as right wing, liberals, etc. I did not mention political parties because a white racist can belong to the Republican, Democratic, or Independent party. White Liberals can also belong to the Republican, Democratic, or Independent party. There appear to be more White that are racist in the Republican Party and more White Liberals in the Democratic Party. The Independents have a diversity of beliefs and opinions.

This book identifies racists compared to liberals not by their words alone, but also by different actions, they perform. Not all Whites are racist and America is a racially mixed country. White men had sex with black slave women and produced millions of children with mixed blood. This interracial sexual activity continued for hundreds of years in America. Moreover, not widely known is the fact that, during slavery, some White women slave owners had sex with Black male slaves.
All children born from Black women impregnated by White men, and possibly some born from White women impregnated by Black men, during slavery were enslaved.

I am blessed and grateful for my wife's support, encouragement, and inspiration. My loving daughter and her husband have also blessed us with wonderful grandchildren, and great-grandchildren. We are grateful for their love and devotion.

Section One

Section One

American History

Ancient History

Politics

American History

American History

America was born when the governing body adopted the Constitution of the United States in 1787. The Constitution was written as a law for the new nation to be governed and, we are often told, to guarantee its people equal protection under the law. However, the original Constitution was ratified by White men, many of whom owned slaves and most of whom either believed in or condoned a slaving society. In fact, slavery was well established in most states at that time. The Constitution was ratified in view of the existence of slavery and written in a manner well calculated to aid and strengthen this crime against humanity. There is an old saying, "truth has nothing to fear," but racist Whites feared the truth in order to continue the sin of slavery.

The Constitution was cunningly devised and wickedly worded not to use such words as "Negroes," "Africans," "slaves" or "slavery." Whenever the subject arose, other words were used including "such persons," "other persons," and "persons held to service or labor." There is a section in the Constitution where it states that if people held to service or labor (referring to slaves) in one state should escape, they must not be freed by the laws of another state.

When the American colonies rebelled from England, Thomas Jefferson was asked to write the Declaration of Independence. Jefferson expressed America's grievances with England and proclaimed America's ideals of freedom and equality. When these words were written, more than 5000,000 Black Americans were slaves.

Jefferson was said to hold more than 100 men and women in bondage while George Washington held hundreds of slaves.

Many Americans realized that slavery was an inhuman practice. However, greed, power, self-satisfaction, and self-righteousness took control of those who were making profits from slavery. Unfortunately, the people in control of government supported the institution of slavery. Despite the freedoms demanded in the Declaration and the freedoms reserved in the Constitution and the Bill of Rights, slavery was not only tolerated in the Constitution, it was codified. The Constitution has been called a living tribute to the art of compromise. That is seen most clearly in the slavery question.

While the word "slavery" is not mentioned in the Constitution, the fact that this document condones or supports slavery can be seen in a few key places. The first is the Enumeration Clause, where representatives are apportioned. Each state is given a number of congressional representatives based on its population. The word "population" includes slaves, which are called "other persons," and then counted as three-fifths of a whole person!

This enumeration was a hard-fought compromise between slave and Free states. Yet, the Free states' advocates did not want slave states to have an advantage of population to claim more representatives. The slave states wanted their slaves to be counted as a whole person for enumeration purposes only. The three-fifths number was a ratio used by Congress in contemporary legislation and was agreed upon with little debate.

In the Constitution the words "no person" instead of any slaves, will be found in section Two. It states, "No person held to be discharged from such service or labor, but shall be delivered upon Claim of the Party to such Service or Labor may be due." In other words, all slaves who escape slavery shall be returned to slavery. This remained the law of the U.S. Constitution in the days before the Civil War.

Despite the anti-slavery sentiments of such "Founding Fathers" as Benjamin Franklin, John Jay, and Patrick Henry, there were no great movements in America to abolish slavery in the nation's first 40 years. The anti-slavery (or abolitionist) movement did not appear until the 1830s with the founding of the American Anti-Slavery Society by William Lloyd Garrison.

Slavery caused a dispute that divided the country and led to the Civil War, and this armed conflict brought the institution to an end in the United States. Two of the great tragedies in American history are the participation of Black people in the Revolutionary War and the Civil War. They fought and died so the nation could prosper. There has not been any recognition or honor paid to them in public schools history books for their service to protect and build this country.

The institution of slavery in the United States divided the country between those who supported slavery and those who were against it. This dispute could only be settled by a civil war between the slave states of the South and the free states of the North. The North went to war against the South after the South withdrew from the Union and attacked the United States in order to maintain a slave society. The northern states were the victors of the Civil War. Under the control of the Republican party, the post-Civil War U.S. government passed new Amendments to the Constitution that removed the divisive practice of slavery from the nation and guaranteed rights for freedmen. Those Amendments are the Thirteenth, ending slavery (1865), the Fourteenth, making Blacks citizens of the United States (1868), and the Fifteenth, prohibiting racial discrimination in voting (1870). (More information on this subject of slavery and the Constitution may be gathered from the following web site which I found to be insightful: http://www.usconstitution.net/consttop_slav.html)

The Civil War and the new Amendments to the Constitution brought joy and hope to Blacks who had been living in America for centuries under inhuman slave conditions. Enslaved Black people and Whites were brainwashed to accept Whites as a superior race having greater intelligence and divine spiritual destiny. With the exception of works written by abolitionists, all American writings at that time portrayed Whites as clean, beautiful, sanctified, and holy. Other American writings portrayed Blacks as savages, evil, dirty, violent, etc. American Whites and Blacks were influenced by distorted history. This type of teaching caused many Whites to resent Blacks newly acquired freedom under the Constitution. Many Whites in the South refused to accept Blacks as their equal and formed organizations to force Blacks into servitude under White rule.

The southern states regain control of their own government after Reconstruction and quickly enacted Black Codes. The new Amendments rendered these Black Codes illegal and established the era of Reconstruction during which African Americans were elected to Congress and state legislatures throughout the South. However, after the Compromise of 1877 and the withdrawal of federal troops from the South ended Reconstruction, new Black Codes were enacted to deny Blacks their right to vote. Many White politicians in the South encouraged terrorist organizations such as the Ku Klux Klan to intimidate Black voters. The Black Codes imposed poll taxes, literacy tests, and other tactics to prevent Blacks from voting. These tactics stopped Blacks from participating in the operation of the United States Government.

The growth of racism, segregation, and unequal law enforcement by southern states and the U. S. government gathered strength from a decision rendered by the U. S. Supreme Court. A case was brought before the Court in 1896 titled, "Plessy v. Ferguson." This is a case that strengthened the advocates of White supremacy, racism, segregation, and the separation of the races.

The case known as Plessy v. Ferguson, 163 U.S. 537 (1869), is recognized as an historic U.S. Supreme Court decision because it upheld the constitutionality of racial segregation under the doctrine of "separate but equal." It was not until 1954 that this doctrine was reversed by the Supreme Court's decision in Brown v. Board of Education.

In 1883, the Supreme Court had ruled in what was known as "the Civil Rights Cases" that the Fourteenth Amendment applied only to the action of government, thereby denying its ability to protect private citizens against discriminatory acts or other infringements of their civil rights. Three years later, the State of Louisiana passed the "Separate Car Act" which mandated separate railway cars for Blacks and Whites on railroads, while stating, however, that such accommodations must be kept "equal." Opposition to the Act arose when a group of Blacks and White citizens in New Orleans formed the Citizens' Committee which was dedicated to the repeal of that law. They prevailed upon Homer Plessy, who was one-eighth Black (then called an "Octoroon)," to be the subject for their test case. By using a subject who could "pass" for White as their plaintiff, the Committee hoped to make it obvious that enforcing racial difference and segregation as a rule of law a travesty of justice.

Though Plessy was actually seven-eighths White, Louisiana law required that he sit in the "colored" cars of railroad trains. On June 7, 1892, Homer Plessy entered a "Whites only" car of the East Louisiana Railroad, sat down and refused to leave. After he was arrested and jailed, the case of Homer Adolph Plessy v. the State of Louisiana was brought before Judge John H. Ferguson. While Plessy claimed that the East Louisiana railroad had denied his rights as a citizen under the Thirteenth and Fourteenth Amendments of the Constitution, Judge Ferguson ruled that the State of Louisiana had the right to regulate railroad companies operating within the state as it saw fit. Plessy then took his case to Louisiana's Supreme Court but this body upheld the decision of Judge Ferguson. The Citizen's Committee shrewdly enlisted noted author and Radical Republican lawyer Albion W. Tourgee to be Plessy's lead counsel in his appeal before the United States Supreme Court in 1896.

The decision came down against Plessy by a vote of 7 to 1 (Justice David Josiah Brewer did not participate). The U.S. Supreme Court found that Louisiana had not violated Plessy's rights under the Fourteenth Amendment. Further, in a majority opinion written by Justice Henry Billings Brown, it was stated, "We consider the underlying fallacy of the plaintiff's argument to consist in the assumption that the enforced separation of the two races stamps the colored race with a badge of inferiority." Justice Brown then added, "Incredibly that if this be so, it is not by reason of anything found in the act, but solely because the colored race chooses to put that construction upon it." (Emphases added). Notice how racist Whites in position of power have misinterpreted laws to rule in their favor and changed the meaning of words.

In the dissent written by lone egalitarian Justice John Marshall Harlan, another view was made clear. Justice Harlan advised, in the eye of the law, there is in this country no superior ruling class of citizens. There is no caste here. Our Constitution is color-blind, and in respect of civil rights, all citizens are equal before the law.

After the Supreme Court ruled in favor of segregation in Plessy, the term "Jim Crow Laws" was popularized to describe laws which separated Whites and blacks in everyday life and denied Blacks the right to vote. By 1920, every former Confederate state had a complete system of Jim Crow Laws and federal offices in the nation's capital had been segregated by Virginia-born President Woodrow Wilson. Jim Crow Laws and the racist climate which was promoted by the Supreme Court's Plessy decision unleashed so-called extra-legal measures such as widespread lynching and other terrorist acts that were committed against Blacks and anyone who spoke out in their defense.

17

(The author is indebted to and directs the reader's attention to more information about this case on the following web page.) http://en.wikipedia.org/wiki/plessy_v._ferguson)

In the Plessy case, the Supreme Court ruled in favor of the "Separate but equal" doctrine. The Court ruled that while Blacks had equal rights under the law, the separation of the races was legal as long as the facilities were equal; however, southern states made no efforts to make their already inferior facilities for Blacks equal to those for Whites. As a result, a Jim Crow system developed under which numerous people were killed and Blacks were denied equal education, accommodations, and the right to vote for several decades.

Interestingly, a future Chief Justice of the Supreme Court, William H. Rehnquist wrote a memo called "A Random Thought on the Segregation Cases" when he was a law clerk for Justice Robert H. Jackson in 1952 during early deliberations that led to the Brown v. Board of Education decision. In his memo Rehnquist argued, "I realized that it is an unpopular and un-humanitarian position, for which I have been excoriated by liberal colleagues but I think Plessy v. Ferguson was right and should be reaffirmed." He added, "in the long run it is the majority who will determine what the constitutional rights of the minority are." In later defending this memo during his Senate confirmation hearing for the position of Chief Justice, Rehnquist slyly tried to blame these ideas on the already deceased Justice Jackson even though Jackson had voted against segregation in Brown! (S. Hgr.99-1067, hearing before the Senate Committee on the Judiciary on the nomination of Justice William Hubbs Rehnquist to be Chief Justice of the United States (July29-31, and August1, 1986).

Here is a telling example of hypocrisy in American jurisprudence during the latter days of Jim Crow. In 1958, Alabama law stated, "It shall be unlawful for White and Colored persons to play together in games, cards, dice, domino, checkers,

18

pool, billiards, softball, basketball, football, golf, track, at swimming pools or any athletic conference." Prejudice extended past the law into the jury box when three White youths who confessed to a Christmas Eve rape of a 17-year old Black girl in Decatur, Georgia were acquitted by the DeKalb County jury.

This is historical American information. Plessy v. Ferguson reinforced the racists' desire to unite against those who wanted equality and integration. White supremacy in the South flourished due to the United States Supreme Court decisions condoning segregation with a camouflaged racist ruling stating "separate but equal" under the law. This concept of "separate but equal" caused many hardships among Black citizens. Their legal rights and voting rights were denied. They were assaulted by White racists and lynched by the Ku Klux Klan with impunity.

Segregation forced Blacks and Liberal Whites to fight for equality and justice for all Americans. A resistance movement against this injustice began to grow stronger as the years progressed. Eventually, this movement forced the Supreme Court to realize segregated laws were counter to the 14th Amendment. These were very violent times in America as the segregation laws against freedom and equality for all Americans began to slowly be repudiated by the courts.

To enforce the 14th Amendment of the Constitution, the Federal Government had to employ National Guardsmen and Federal Marshals to protect citizens exercising their rights under the Constitution. The Civil Rights Act and Voting Rights Act were passed in 1946 and 1965, respectively, ending legalized segregation and disenfranchisement, thus removing Jim Crow by law.

Racism and prejudice still exist in America today because of the distorted history taught within some families as well as in schools, the mainstream media, and movies. There is much work to be done to educate Americans with true historical facts of ancient Africa and the entirety of American history. Racism in America will continue to diminish, as Americans understand the true history of Africans and the contributions of all races working together for a united America.

The following is a part of America's history that should be discussed and taught in our public schools. This is important history for African Americans who need to be informed of their contributions in making America a strong nation. True knowledge will enhance African Americans' pride when they are fully aware of their place in American history. This information will also give Black Americans a variety of subjects to discuss pertaining to their history, especially since it goes beyond slavery.

Native Americans (once known as Indians) also suffered the White race's invasion of their territory. When Europeans arrived in this land now called America, they were received by Indians as friends. Whites continued to arrive in this land of America and their numbers grew. This growth encouraged them to expand their communities into "Indian Territory." Indians resisted White invasion of their territory. That era is known as the Indian Wars. Many Indians were massacred and their villages were destroyed. Whites were better armed and, as a consequence of many years of war, Whites defeated the Indians and confined them to live on barren lands called Indian reservations. Regarding suppressed information about Native Americans and the historical African American fight for freedom, one should consult this site: http//www.johnhorse.com/black-seminole-slave-rebellion.htm; pay particular attention to the section called, "The slave rebellion the country tried to forget."

As the author of the above web site wrote in conclusion, "it remains something of a mystery how the country's largest slave rebellion has remain unrecognized...even by the country's leading scholars of African American studies." While it is true that rebellions and other acts of resistance by the enslaved have traditionally been underreported by American historians, the size of this rebellion begs one to speculate as to why.

During the Second Seminole War (1835-1842), enslaved Blacks joined in battle with both Seminole Indians and Black Seminoles, the Africans who had escaped from slavery and were living among or were allies of the Seminole Indians. Their opponents were U.S. troops in Florida who were trying to expel the Seminoles and make Florida safer for slavery. In 1836, at the height of this war for self-determination, at least 385 slaves (and possibly more than 500) successfully carried out a plan to destroy more than 21 sugar plantations in Florida with the help of their Black and Indian Seminole allies. The enslaved then escaped to freedom, most of them staying on with the Seminoles to live and to do battle against U.S. forces.

One wonders if the reason for this almost 175-year-long oversight has something to do with the idea that American, slavery could not have been so cruel that hundreds of slaves were simultaneously driven to conspire and rise up in rebellion against it and chose to live among Indians to escape it. Or is the image of slave combatants burning plantations to the ground and warring against White-led government forces only acceptable when speaking of foreign Blacks, such as those in the Haitian Revolution? Or is it that revolt flies in the face of long-held stereotype of docile American slaves who could rarely be convinced to rebel with arms against their masters, let alone join in a war against their masters' nation? Or maybe it is all of the above.

African American Westward Expansion

African American Westward Expansion

American history is often written to describe Native Americans as savages and the Whites as crusaders, bringing civilization and humanity to a lowly race of people. As the population of the White race increased in great numbers, they began to expand their empire westward into Native American land. Particularly in the post-Civil War era, African Americans also journeyed west with the hope of finding a new home by escaping from racism. African Americans played a major part in the westward expansion of the United States from the beginnings.

Thomas Jefferson made the transaction called the Louisiana Purchase with France in the year 1803. President Jefferson wanted the northern part of this land and other western lands to be surveyed. He hired Meriwether Lewis and William Clark to accomplish that job. William Clark owned a slave called York, a skilled hunter who spoke several languages including French. York had good communication with the Indians which was helpful to Lewis and Clark when passing through Indian Territory. Their expedition was completed in the year 1806. William Clark granted York his freedom after their expedition.

The prospect of westward expansion of American territory created a national excitement. African Americans were among those who traveled westward to improve their conditions, and some escaped from slavery in order to accomplish it. Many slaves knew how to hunt, build cabins, and farm the land; some also knew how to negotiate with the Indians. Many Blacks were admitted into Indian Nations (also known as Tribes). Some Blacks married Indian women, raised families with them, and lived in Indian villages. On many occasions, they protected

Whites from angry Indians by diplomacy. Many slaves were granted their freedom for their help in saving the lives of their masters.

Many African Americans who integrated with the Indians became known as Black Indians. Some Blacks were recognized as chiefs of some Indian villages. One of those Blacks was James Beckwourth. Beckwouth was a hunter and scout for the U.S. Army during the Seminole War. He also found a passageway through the Sierra Nevada mountain range near Reno, Nevada. This discovery helped future settlers to reach California. That pass is now called Beckwourth Pass. Blacks were also involved in the California Gold Rush as they were looking for freedom and riches. The settlement of the West was an issue that played a major part in bringing the slavery debate up front in the halls of American government.

Among the national issues and debates which concerned westward expansion and slavery were:
1.   The Missouri Compromise of 1820
2.   States' Rights
3.   The Webster-Hayne Debate
4.   The Calhoun Resolution
5.   Nullification
6.   The Wilmot Proviso
7.   The Free-Soil Coalition
8.   Popular Sovereignty or Squatter Sovereignty
9   The Fugitive Slave Act of 1850
10.   The Compromise of 1850
11.   The Kansas-Nebraska Act

All of these conflicts and policies led to the Civil War. It was the defeat of the Confederate Army and Reconstruction under the Republican Party, and not the original Constitution of the United States written by the "Founding Fathers" who counted slaveholders among their ranks, that dealt a mortal blow to the institution of slavery. The victors of the Civil War passed laws to free slaves. Those laws included the 13th Amendment passed in 1865, abolished slavery in the United States and its territories, the 14th Amendment granted citizenship to African Americans in 1868, and the 15th Amendment was added in 1870 that made it illegal to deny the right to vote based upon one's race. (This applied only to male citizens as women of all colors at that time were denied the right to vote).

The United States Congress also established the Freedmen's Bureau. The full name of this agency was Bureau of Refugees, Freedmen and Abandoned Lands. This Bureau was established to provide protection for former slaves and help them find paying jobs and places to live until they could adjust to this newfound freedom. Schools were set up in most states for Black Americans. All help and consideration for the new freedom for Blacks came to a close after the Compromise of 1877 and Rutherford B. Hayes became president. White southerners regained control and passed Jim Crow laws which took freedom and equality from Blacks. The reign of terror returned for Black Americans. This terror drove many of them westward, hoping for a better life and independence. They have played a major part in developing the western part of the country.

Black men worked as cattle drivers, cooks, miners, railroad workers, and fur traders. Some became farmers, and others were hired as unskilled laborers and service workers. There were also Black western deputy marshals/lawmen and cowboys. Black women were also a part of this inclusive history. They worked all sorts of jobs as women of the west. They worked as domestics, farm workers, seamstresses, innkeepers, cooks, laundresses, schoolteachers, general store operators, Sunday school teachers, and nurses. Many also went westward as "mail-order brides." Blacks were depending upon their own creative abilities. By 1920, over fifty towns had been settled by them in the west. Many Blacks were living in towns across Oklahoma. President Benjamin Harrison had begun the Land Rush of 1889

24

by issuing a proclamation which stated, "The public Lands in Oklahoma District are opened to settlers on April 22, 1889." More than 60,000 Native Americans had been forced from southeastern states during the 1830's by U.S. troops. They were forced westward to Oklahoma, Kansas, and Nebraska. The Indians were led on a forced march known as the "Trail Of Tears." Blacks served as solders in the westward expansion of the country. The Native Americans called them "Buffalo Soldiers" because of their fighting strength and tightly curled hair, which was said to resemble the mighty Buffalo of the Great Plains. One mission for the Buffalo Soldiers was to keep "Boomers" off lands not assigned to them. Oklahoma was designated as part Indian Territory, but the Boomers kept coming.

The 9th Cavalry of the Buffalo Soldiers kept the unassigned land clear since it had been set aside as places for reestablishing a new homeland for Native Americans. They protected other settlers as their wagon trains moved westward. Buffalo Soldiers were active peacemakers when angry Native Americans were thinking of making war against the settlers during the 1880's. Buffalo Soldiers protected mail routes and railroad surveyors during this period. These soldiers were stationed at Fort Reno in El Reno, Oklahoma.

To find information pertaining to this subject search the web about African American westward Expansion etc. and also African American historical participations.

In the late 1800's, it is likely that Black Cowboys made up 25% of the West's cowhands and other colorful men of the range. These cattle handlers, horsemen, and roving free spirits included: Bill Pickett, a great rodeo man who would jump from his horse, wrestle a full-grown steer to the ground, and then bite and hold the steer's nose and lip until it was still. This practice earned Bill Pickett the name "Bulldogger." With his brothers, Pickett created "The Pickett Brothers Bronco Busters and rough Riders

Association," and he participated in rodeos and Wild West Shows all over North and South America and even Europe.

Bass Reeves counted himself among the hundreds of U.S. marshals who were appointed to keep the peace in the Old West. Black lawmen of the West were not a great rarity, and others included Ben Boyer of Coaldale, Colorado; Francis T. Bruce of Denver, Colorado; Rufus Cannon of Fort Smith, Oklahoma; Robert I. Fortune of Wilburton, Oklahoma; Grant Johnson of Eufaula, Oklahoma; and George Winston of Fort Smith, Oklahoma.

If there were Black lawmen then there had to be Black outlaws, and among these were: Rufus Buck of Okmulgee, Oklahoma; Crawford Goldsby, aka Cherokee Bill of Fort Concho, Texas; Ben Hodges of the infamous Dodge City, Kansas; Ned Huddleston, aka Isom Dart; and Buss Luckey of Columbus, Ohio.

Notable Black women of the Old West included:
Clara Brown who owned a laundry in Central City, Colorado which was frequented by miners. By the mid-1860's, she had become a wealthy woman; she was very religious, hosting Methodist church meetings in her home and using much of her wealth to help the needy, particularly those who had once been enslaved as she had been. Before her death, she was reunited with her daughter Eliza Jane who had been torn from her during slavery.

Mary Fields, aka "Stagecoach Mary" who worked as a mail courier, driving a stagecoach for eight years. She wore a man's hat and coat while doing so.

Biddy Mason of California, like Clara Brown in Colorado, was a wealthy black woman known for helping the needy. She was a well-known philanthropist who gave aid to poor people of all

races. Ms. Mason also was a founder of the First African
Methodist Episcopal Church of Los Angeles in 1872.
Mary Ellen Pleasant, a businesswoman and civil rights activist in
California, fought and won cases against segregation in the
1860's.

Another important Black settler of the West was Edwin P.
McCabe, a man who had served as the state auditor in Kansas for
four years and as the state auditor in Oklahoma for ten years. He
once decided to purchase 320 acres of land and from that
beginning later established the town of Langston, Oklahoma in
1890. He named the town after John Mercer Langston, who was
the first Black Congressman elected from Virginia. Mr. McCabe
set aside forty acres of land which provided for the Land Grant
College called Oklahoma Colored Agricultural and Normal
University in 1897. The university was later renamed Langston
University in 1941.

Despite the efforts of forward-thinking individuals such as
McCabe, great tragedy would befall the African community of
Tulsa, Oklahoma in 1921. From 1900 to 1921, the Greenwood
district of Tulsa, Oklahoma was a thriving Black community
often referred to as the "Negro Wall Street" of America. The
African American developer O.W. Gurley had started this
community which eventually comprised businesses, private
homes, churches, and other institutions. The death knell of Black
Wall Street began with a comparatively insignificant incident.
On May 30, 1921, a young Black shoeshine worker was accused
of assaulting a young White woman in an elevator.

Although charges would later be dropped against the accused,
and he would escape Tulsa to safety, on May 31, 1921, a White
Tulsa lynch mob started one of the worst race riots in American
history. Over two days of rioting, at least dozens of blacks were
killed compared to about 10 Whites killed. In the Greenwood
district over thousands of homes own by African Americans
were destroyed by White inflamed racist hatred, jealousy, and

27

envy of a successful prosperous Black town. To make matters worse in the waning hours of this tragedy, airplanes bombed this town and National Guardsmen rounded up Black men in an effort to quell the violence. There were no charges against the White invaders killing and destroying of a peaceful, successful black town of Greenwood in Tulsa, Oklahoma.

Influencing American Minds

Influencing American Minds

During my young childhood, I attended American public schools. The history I was taught consisted mainly of European, and American History. I was taught Native Americans (Indians) were savages and Africans were people from a primitive culture and continent. I was also taught that Europeans occupied Africa to bring the "natives" Christianity and to civilize them. In American history classes, I learned that Blacks were enslaved here at the same time politicians were proclaiming that America was a free country. Fortunately, I was also taught that there were disputes between Whites who believed in slavery and Whites who were against it, and that these disputes led to the War Between the States.

In my youth, I was also constantly exposed to pictures of Jesus Christ as a White man with blond hair and blue eyes. Hollywood movies, and media, etc. presented all Christian subjects as having originated from White substance and orientations. Such works excluded Blacks as if they were not involved in any manner with or had any participation in developing those beliefs.

They claimed Africans were heathens, savages, and worshipped idols and had no knowledge of God. That was part of my young education as a Black child growing up in America. I ask the reader to imagine the effect that type of education must have on the mind of a child of mostly African descent and on that of a child of mostly European descent. This type of teaching causes a problem between the races as a result of distorted facts.

The schools continue to teach untruths about history in order to condone support of White racism, savagery, slavery, and injustice. An accurate view of history will show that White Americans have committed crimes which some schoolbooks have accused African and Native Americans of performing. This is one of the reasons I state it is past time for Black Americans to take charge of the education of their children and teach them true ancient African history and culture, and true American history as well.

African American scholars, teachers, and parents should teach their children they are direct descendants of the greatest and proudest race on the face of this earth. Black Americans need to be taught Black pride and that Black is beautiful. The White race has taught themselves White pride and "White is beautiful." My problem with the White race is its distortion of African civilization and culture.

During ancient times, Africans built the pyramids and, even today, so-called modern man cannot fathom how they built them. It is obvious that Egyptian Sphinx have African features. Notice that some of these features, such as the broad nose and thick lips, have been removed by hostile Europeans.

The story of religion started in Africa. Africa is the birthplace of religious beliefs such as monotheism---a belief in one god alone---that was copied by Europeans. Europeans that controlled government in the Dark Ages later denounced Europeans who accepted African spiritual beliefs that were spreading among their population. That denunciation was a major incentive for spiritual beliefs to grow stronger among Europeans.

When the European rulers realized they could not stop the growth of African spiritual beliefs among their race, they adopted those beliefs but with their own interpretations of them. The Europeans interpreted the African spiritual beliefs in many ways to promote their agenda. A well-known example of many different interpretations of spiritual beliefs is the King James Version of the Bible. Blacks should take on the responsibility of educating their own children about their history and not relinquish that job to others. I do not have to point out what the results were from distorting Black History. Unfortunately, distorting facts and history have encouraged many Blacks to believe in White privilege, White control, and White rule. Blacks have to be aware of White racists and backward-thinking Blacks whom I will refer to as 'Negroes."

Throughout this nation's history, racists and Negroes have not stopped African Americans and liberal Whites from fighting for freedom and equality. This is the day and time for American Blacks to unite in the knowledge of the proud history of their ancestors. Learning of their true history will give them a better appreciation and knowledge of who started humanity's awareness of spiritual knowledge and beliefs. Knowledge of true history is important for a race of people to understand where they came from, and who they truly are, and what role they played in the development of humanity. Africans are the first people to operate in high levels of science, architecture, medicine, mathematics, astronomy, spirituality, etc.

The oldest records of the beginning of civilization were discovered in Ancient Africa. From the beginning of time, Africa was the land of the black and brown people, and it was also the central gathering place for the entire world. Africans were described in ancient times by Europeans as Moors and Africa was called Ethiopia by Europeans. Africa played a major role in the development of world civilization with knowledge that is used today. Great teachers and philosophers of Africa were teaching science, medicine, and the arts throughout ancient times and even as late as the period of the Transatlantic Slave Trade, an era which some refer to as "the Black Holocaust."

Ancient African History

Ancient African History

I have discovered a web site on the Internet that has valuable historical information about the continent of Africa, the Black African race, and other races. I will transcribe historical information from this site because there is more to history besides a European version. There are different written views about history because all races in this world have contributed to civilization. The Europeans' version would lead one to think they are the only ones to promote the civilization of the human race. That is clearly untrue, as evidence I offer among other facts, contained in the following web site: http://stewartsynopsis.com/blacked_out_through_whitewash.htm This site has much historical information is titled, "Blacked out through Whitewash." I recommend this site for presenting the involvement of all races in shaping the destiny of humanity. This site will be paraphrased by me. Note that this site states, "Because the need is critical, this book may be copied and distributed. Sections of this book can be copied as long as credit is given to the book's author." The authors name is, Suzar.

This site starts with explanations of religious development, spiritual beliefs, spiritual journeys, and shows Blacks to be the original believers in one God. Different religions developed over centuries because of diversity of humans and different interpretations of scriptural writings. The site mentions descriptions of biblical men with African hair and features. There are people of color in the Bible too, not just people of the White race as the European version of the Bible will encourage you to believe.

At the beginning of history, Blacks were the only inhabitants of the continent of Africa; Whites were the only inhabitants of the continent of Europe; Asians inhabited the continent of Asia; and Native Americans inhabited the American continents. Africa is where the Garden of Eden was located. Spiritual beliefs and awareness started in Africa. Africans are a race of people with brown and black skins, woolly hair, wide noses, and full lips, as displayed in the art of the ancient Egyptians in Africa. This art is proof of the features of African people in ancient times. Europeans have tried to destroy or deface statues of ancient times that have African features. The people of the earth traveled, mingled, and integrated with each other for centuries. This integration has changed the original look of people from countries and regions since the beginning of time. (End of paraphrase).

I will quote two full sections from this site as well:
Section One
Ancient Egypt was a Black African Civilization.
The ancient Egyptians called themselves Kam or Kam-Au (black people/Black God-people), and their country Kamit or Kemet, both meaning land of the Blacks and the Black land. The word Egypt is derived from the Greek word Aigyptos (or Aiguptos) that means Black! Europe's first historian, Herodotus, said, "The Egyptians, Colchains, and Ethiopians have thick lips, and broad nose, woolly hair and they have burnt skin. Egyptian civilization evolved from the Ethiopians." The Bible equates Ham (Africans) with Egypt. (Ps. 78:51, 105:23, 27, 106: 21, 22).

The Black identity of Egyptian mummies is proven by their high melanin content. Also, Egyptians made wigs from sheep wool to match their woolly hair! A superb summary of the first Egyptians, their culture & achievements is documented in Legrand Clegg's video "Egypt during the Golden Age." Other great works include Gerald Massey's scholarly "Egypt, Light of the World" and James Brunson's "Predynastic Egypt." Ra Un

33

Nefer Amen presents a powerful synthesis of the esoteric sciences of ancient Egypt, India & Canaan in "Metu Neter."

Section two
Whites blew off the Africoid nose of the Sphinx, and destroyed much ancient Africoid art. Carved from a single rock, the Sphinx was a portrait of the Black Pharaoh, Khafre (Cephren)...a blatant, undeniable evidence of Black African achievements...(Jealous Europeans) blew off the Africoid nose and parts of the lips with cannon fire! Reporting on the "riddle" of the racial identity of the ancient Egyptians, Count C. Volney, a distinguished French scholar who visited Egypt in the late 1700's has written with astonishment, "when I visited the Sphinx, its appearance gave me the key to the riddle. Beholding that head typically Negro in all its features..." He later added, "...the Egyptians are true Negroes of the same type as all native-born Africans." The Sphinx's broad nose and full lips are evident in an early drawing of the Sphinx as it was found in the 19th century.

The willful and systematic destruction of Africoid art has also occurred in the Americas, Asia and India: inscriptions and hieroglyphics are defaced or bleached, noses are shot off or chiseled down, and confusing nomenclatures are pasted over the evidence. Photos are taken from misleading angles or filters, and some evidence is outright destroyed. Europeans replaced the African inscriptions with new ones that credit themselves for the achievement.

The heroes & people of the Bible were primarily Black African people. Moses was an Egyptian priest (Ex. 4: 6, 7). Black Sampson had dreadlocks. Solomon declares, "I am black," as does Job: "My skin is black." (Sol. 1:6, Job 30: 30). Simon was a Canaanite (Mt. 10: 4). Paul was mistaken for an "Egyptian" (Acts 21: 37-39). Seeking to further discredit African legacy, White historians try to displace Egypt from Africa by classifying it as part of Asia, but the ancient people of West Asia were also Black.

The original people of West Asia were the Sumerians, who called themselves the 'Black-Heads." They founded the rich Black cultures of Mesopotamia that included the ancient Babylonians, Chaldeans, Canaanites, Phoenicians and Elamites (original Persians). Cush or Nubia means Ethiopia. The Biblical table of nations (Gen. 10) tells us that Cush and Canaan were brothers (sons of Ham), and that Sumer (Shina) is descended from Cush. Old Testament compliers assign Ham (father of Africans) to Egypt, Canaan, Cush, and Phut (Libia). The Bible refers to Egypt as Ham. (Ps. 78:51; 105:23, 27; 106; 21, 22) (End of Section quotes)

The above information is very interesting and gives some new topics to wonder about when considering how events evolved over centuries on earth. It is important to know the participations of Africans in the Bible scriptures presented to the world.

Ancient African religion is the foundation of Christianity in Europe. The Europeans interpret the Bible using European names and symbols. They have removed all traces of African names, references to scenery and maps pertaining to anything that is of African involvement.

British and American governments have always distorted historical information relating to Africans and their participation in the development of civilization, spiritual beliefs, and Black American contributions to American history. Africans were written out of ancient history, religion, and science, and were not recognized as innovators and inventors.

American Blacks were brainwashed for hundreds of years while living in America under forced slave labor. In America, they were forced to exit under the worst conditions of man's inhumanity to man. Yet, this savage condition existed in a country that prides itself as a country of freedom and equality for its entire people. European Whites dehumanized African Blacks in order to legitimize their inhuman treatment of the Black race. They have rewritten history, stating Blacks are a savage and primitive people that practice cannibalism. They have also reinterpreted scriptures by stating they (Whites) were commanded by God to bring religion to the Blacks and educate them because that was their humanitarian duty. These Whites will not mention how they forced Blacks into slavery, and even separated children from parents by selling them for money as if they were merchandise and not human beings.

American racists have brainwashed Whites and Blacks that white skin, straight blond hair, and blue eyes are beautiful. Americans also are brainwashed that dark skin, woolly hair, and full lips are ugly. That doctrine of "Black is ugly" has been published and preached for generations in the media, movies, schools, and via beauty pageants. Racist have espoused that everything white in color is pure and beautiful.

White- controlled businesses in America manufactured White dolls exclusively as late as the mid-Twentieth Century. Black parents could only purchase White dolls for their children to play with. By loving White dolls, African American children negatively impacted their own self-esteem. After the insistence by Black parents that Black dolls should also be manufactured; Black children still preferred White dolls to the Black ones because of White brainwashing that Black is ugly and White is beautiful. Even grown Black adults were influenced by such brainwashing. Whites continue their brainwashing to include a spiritual conception by stating that the Lord Jesus Christ has white skin, blond hair, and blue eyes.

The area where Jesus was raised was Africa, a land of Blacks. During ancient times, Blacks were the inhabitants of Africa and Whites inhabited Europe. Whites have written Blacks out of the Bible and out of religion. It is important for Black Americans and White Americans to learn the truth of all races' involvement

36

in history. This will help to break down barriers and promote unity and understanding between humans.

It is helpful to know and understand there is no race more superior or better than any other. The educational system of the United States was designed to exclude Black Americans from advancing in America society. Racists in control wanted to build up the self-esteem of the White race and destroy the self- esteem of the Black race. The American educational system portrayed Africans and Blacks in a negative light. Blacks need true information about their history in order to give them self-confidence, high self-esteem and proud "race esteem." American schools should present true American history with true African American participation in America's development.

American schools should emphasize the multi-cultural participations of the diverse racial and ethnic groups which have made this a prosperous country. There is an inhuman historical fact in America that some racists still believe the Bible justifies slavery. Many priests and pastors owned slaves. These are religious believers that did not see the evil of slavery. During the 1800s, there were racist church leaders who used the Bible to defend slavery. Such church officials distorted the meaning of the passages from the New Testament in order to convince others to accept their racist beliefs. Here are some Biblical scriptures used by ministers to condone and legitimize the institution of slavery:

1. Ephesians, Chapter 6, verses 5 to 9, starting with, "Servants, be obedient to them that are your Masters;"
2. 1 Timothy, Chapter 6, verses 1 to 7, starting with, "Let as many servants as are under the yoke count their Masters worthy;"
3. 1 Peter, Chapter 2, verses 18 to 25, starting with, "Servants be subject to your Masters with all fear."

Those religious leaders who owned slaves and had sex with them were not recognized as sinners by their religion. That is proof Blacks were not accepted as humans. Some believe they were expressing their faith by claiming kindness to their slaves. However, not all Christian leaders condoned or supported slavery. Slavery was denounced by many Christian leaders as evil. The passing of the Thirteenth Amendment to the United States Constitution in 1865 outlawed slavery. The true teaching of the Bible finally prevailed that all humans are created equal and are not property of one another.

Blacks must take back control of their minds and study their true history. This is a challenge of the mind and spirit that Black people need to face in order to overcome the lies which have led to physical and mental enslavement. It is great to know however, that there are many Blacks who were not brainwashed to believe the many lies that have been told about Africa, its people, and their descendants here in America. There have been many great Africans and African American historians and scholars who have known the importance of learning and teaching true history so people of the world may understand the many contributions of different cultures and races. White supremacy has propagandized that White culture was the start of civilization while dehumanizing the achievements of African civilizations.

An article written by African scientist and historian Cheikh Anta Diop and African American historian and educator Dr. John Henrik Clarke was once found on this web site which is now defunct: (http://www.thepatrioticvangard.com/article.php3?id_article=90 3). The title of their article was, "Africa is the Cradle of Civilization." I will now paraphrase their article.
African culture played a significant role in influencing the development of science, mathematics, and other intellectual disciplines, thereby advancing the pursuit of civilization around the world. The oldest set of human bones on this planet was found in Africa. It has been stated throughout history that Black people are the original people of this planet. The original people on earth were dark-skin people from a place commonly known as kemet by Black scholars.

Ancient African civilization consisted of knowledge and wisdom so powerful it was a paradigm for many others which followed. African people were spiritually minded and their spirituality led them to build great temples with beautiful ancient artifacts within as well as such wonders of the world as the Pyramids and the Sphinx. Europeans were amazed of those structures; many are still wondering how Africans were able to build those tremendous monuments. Europeans were very impressed with African structures. They attempted to give those structures the appearance of European heritage. They chipped away African features of the Sphinx to hide the apparent connection to the Black race. Many European scholars have even claimed that Egypt was a European civilization. Many Europeans have either ignored or distorted African wonders of the world and will not accept Africa as the home of spirituality and higher learning. Ultimately, they had to agree that Egypt and all ancient civilizations along the Nile were Africa populated by Black people until the integration of the African continent by Europeans. Some of the ancient African civilizations that existed in Africa were Ghana, Mali and Songhai. Many African Civilizations were destroyed by European invasions which resulted in force slavery and colonialism.

African nations were great traders among themselves and European nations. Europeans were mystified at the beauty of Africa and the efficiency in which they governed their land and people. Europeans defeated and conquered the Africans through lethal weaponry, slavery, and sowing divisions among African people. They spread the evil practice of slavery in West Africa and then forced colonialism on many African people while robbing the continent of its riches and history. Europeans have told the greatest lie to cover up their inhumanity to man by claiming they were civilizing the African continent.
Africans were living in a state of peace in tune with nature when European aggression came from the Romans in 332 BC.

39

Whenever true history is exposed, the truth is then known that an African named Imhotep was the father of medicine, not the Greek Hippocrates. There have been reports that Hippocrates wrote that he was a student of the great Imhotep. Historical proof has been presented of early African presence in every culture on earth.

Many lies have spread from generation to generation, promoting White supremacy and degrading Blacks and their culture. These lies are used to spread the deceitful propaganda that Whites are intellectually and morally superior to blacks. (End of paraphrase)

In this country, Black females have been brainwashed to believe light skin is prettier than dark skin and that long, straight, light-colored hair is prettier than Afro or shorter curly dark hair. White skin can become sunburned under too much sun. Black skin is protected from sunburn. Europeans, stringy hair can easily become a home for lice insects. Whites will not admit that lice are attracted to their hair. For many years, Whites have used suntan lotions to darken their skin. They have used beauty contests to promote their skin, features, and hair as beautiful. They have used the media and movies to brainwash Americans that White is beautiful and Black is ugly. For decades, beauty contests were for White women only. During integration, they permitted Black females to participate and some have won the contest. All the Blacks who have won had such European features as light skin and long stringy hair. These beauty contests promoted the White agenda. No female with dark skin having an Afro hairdo was permitted to participate.

White people have that right to glamorize their race; my objection is that they also dehumanize the Black race. Black people are the only ones capable of promoting Black Beauty as Whites have promoted White Beauty. There are many beautiful, Black, dark-skin females with afro hairdos. Blacks need to promote Black Beauty. That is one of their greatest challenges after centuries of brainwashing.

They should constantly repeat to themselves and their children that their darker skin is beautiful, and that their Afro hair is beautiful. Dark-skin females can see how beautiful their skin color is in conjunction with brightly worn colors. Their skin tone glamorizes bright colors. With her pretty brown complexion, First Lady Michelle Obama is a perfect role model to display her skin's beauty with the pretty colors she wears. A Black beauty contest would play a major role in promoting Black beauty and convincing many Black females and males that they need to remove hundreds of years of brainwashing from their minds. Beauty should be in the eyes of the beholder, but if the eyes of the beholder have been brainwashed for centuries, those eyes may believe only White is beautiful. White skin is beautiful, and Black skin is also beautiful. During the protest of the late 1960s, there was a song by James Brown that the people sang in the streets, "Say it loud, I'm Black and I'm Proud."

Racial Symbols and Code Words

Racial Symbols and Code Words

Racist symbols are burning crosses by racist Whites dressed in white sheets and hoods to cover their faces, a hangman's rope with noose attached, and a Nazi Swastika.

Racist Code Words:
Mainstream America (meaning White America)
Right-wingers (meaning mostly White people)
Supporting western culture (believing in White supremacy)
Middle America (meaning mostly White people)
Suburbia (meaning White neighborhoods)
Middle class (meaning mostly White people)
Upper class (meaning mostly rich White people)
Christian Fundamentalists (meaning White people)
Left-wingers (meaning Black people and White people who support equality for all Americans)
Cities or towns (meaning neighborhoods, often of many races)
Inner cities (meaning Black neighborhoods)
Ghetto (meaning Black neighborhoods)
Poorer or lower class (meaning mostly Black people)
Slums (meaning Black and other non-White neighborhoods)

The reason the above statements are labeled racist code words is because this country is divided racially and its media uses "code words" to report biased news pertaining to particular groups. Certain mob violence involving Blacks is reported as a group problem instigated and caused by that group; the media usually labels these events "riots." When reporting mass incidents, the mainstream media either singles out for criticism or praises group members depending on what race is involved in these actions. Reporting about White violent incidents is usually

42

downplayed as a rare occurrence. Reports on Black violent incidents are usually blown up or portrayed as frequent occurrences in Black neighborhoods.

How to identify a dedicated right-wing person:
Right-winger is a person that will preach he knows what is the right way for people to act, what to believe in, how they should live their lives, what laws to obey or disobey, when to protest and what to protest about. A right-winger's attitude is you must not dispute them because only they know what is right or wrong. When you have a dispute with a right-winger and you do not answer their questions their way, they will interrupt you, disagree with you and rephrase the question in order to force a response that will satisfy their criteria and their beliefs.

Right-wingers believe in self-glory, riches, power, and self-benefit. They will not hesitate to put labels they believe are degrading on anyone who does not agree with their ideas or beliefs. They believe in self-help, self-support, and self-achievement without any type of intervention or support from anyone or any government. Right-wingers believe in White power, White control, and White privileges--even if they are actually non-White.

How to identify a dedicated liberal:
Liberal believes in working together to promote opportunities for a community, people, or any project that will help to bring unity and cooperation. A liberal will disagree with respect for others' opinions, beliefs or ideas. They will let you express your ideas or opinions without interruption. They believe in working together to help people of all colors and faiths as well as people in need. Liberal believes in sharing. They will take under consideration other opinions and ideas. Liberals understand they are not perfect and can be incorrect at times, and they are willing to listen and weigh evidence presented in order to make partial changes or a complete change. They will not label people who will not agree with them. They respect people of all races and religions and

43

believe in equal justice and opportunities for everyone. Right-wingers, in this new day and time, recognize liberals as a legitimate socio-political faction; in the old days, White people with liberal beliefs were labeled "Niger lovers" by racist Whites.

Word descriptions of certain Blacks by other Blacks: There are American Blacks who do not believe there is a racial problem in America or that there are racist Whites who strive to control and stop Black Americans from achieving unity. Some also believe there is no unjust law imposed on the Black race in America. They have aligned themselves with White control and White rule, and many African Americans have branded them "Negros." A Negro can be exposed when he believes in and supports White control and argues against African American protest and complaints about injustices and denials of equal opportunity.

A Negro is also identified by his ridicule of Black leaders that lead protest marches. Negroes does not support obtaining justice for Blacks; he does not believe it is a problem. Negroes only blame Blacks for crimes, school dropouts, unemployment, and run-down neighborhoods. They will not support any argument that will improve African American schools, communities, employment, or equal justice. They will put all the blame on African Americans and not on racism or unfairness in the judicial system.

People are destroyed because of lack of knowledge. Internet web sites controlled by Blacks have played a major role in presenting their side of events plus any violations of their rights. Black web sites inform people of their history and coming events to be observed. African web sites are observant of injustices and civil rights violations, etc. Unbiased information is vital for Black Americans; they must also be aware of right-wing racist reporting about Blacks. After the Civil War and the Emancipation of African Americans, policies were enacted during what is known as the "Reconstruction Era" to help Black

Americans adjust to freedom and allow the southern states to rejoin the Union. During this period of Reconstruction, there were many Black politicians and administrators. Many Scholars have identified more than 1,500 Black office holders during the Reconstruction period. All were members of the Republican Party, the party of Lincoln.

The following are names of some Black office holders after the Civil War:
1. Blanche K. Bruce, U.S. Senator from Mississippi
2. Tunis Campbell, State Senator from Georgia
3. Robert B. Elliot, State house lawmaker and U.S. Representative from South Carolina
4. Jonathan Clarkson Gibbs, Secretary of State and Secretary of Public instruction of Florida
5. Mufflin Wistar Gibbs, Arkansas judge and the younger brother of Jonathan Clarkson Gibbs
6. Thomas Van Renssalaer Gibbs, Member, Florida House of Representatives and son of Jonathan Clarkson Gibbs
7. John Mercer Langston, first African-American elected to the U.S. Congress from Virginia, and first African-American to hold elected office in U.S. history (Township Clerk in Ohio)
8. James D. Lynch, Secretary of State of Mississippi
9. John R. Lynch, Member, Mississippi House of Representatives, elected to U.S. House of Representatives
10. Samuel A. McElwee, Member, Tennessee General Assembly
11. Robert Meacham, Florida State Senator
12. John Willis Menard, first African American elected to the U.S. Congress (denied his seat)
13. Charles H. Pearce, Member, Florida Senate
14. P.B.S. Pinchback, Governor of Louisiana
15. Joseph Hayne Rainey, U.S. Representative from South Carolina, member of the South Carolina Senate, and first African American to serve in the U.S. House of Representatives
16. James T. Rapier, Member, United States House of Representatives
17. Hiram R. Revels, U.S. Senator from Mississippi, and first

African American to serve in either House of Congress
18. Robert Smalls, South Carolina Representative, South Carolina Senator, U.S. Representative
19. Josiah T. Walls, U.S. Representative
The previous information may also be found on this web page: http://en.wikipedia.org/wiki/List_of_African-American_officeholders_during_Reconstruction.

Racist Whites will not allow the complete, true American history to be taught in schools, shown in movies, or other media, or even discussed in public forums if it is up to them. This is a part of history racists do not want Americans to know. They will ignore the problems that engulf America and promote America as a free and open society with liberty and justice for all, that theme is taught in American schools, media, movies and history books, etc. The worst parts of America's past and present are ignored and downplayed as a problem that will be solved by American determination; however, that can only happen when racists no longer have any control.

List of Influential Blacks

List of Influential Blacks

Here is a partial list of influential Blacks that currently participate in all fields including politics, law, business, religion, arts and entertainment, education, and public service. This list is to inform the reader of dedicated leaders of their community and country.

Politics and Law: 1. U.S. Rep. John Conyers, Jr. (Michigan)
2. U.S. Rep. Elijah E. Cummings (Maryland)
3. U.S. Rep. Eleanor Holmes Norton (Congressional Delegate, Washington D.C.)
4. U.S. Rep. Jesse L. Jackson, Jr. (Illinois)
5. U.S. Rep. Sheila Jackson-Lee (Texas)
6. U.S. Rep. John Lewis (Georgia)
7. U.S. President Barack Obama
8. U.S. Rep. Charles Rangel (New York)
9. U.S. Rep. Maxine Waters (California)
10. Governor Deval Patrick (Massachusetts)
11. Governor Douglas Wilder (Virginia, and former Mayor of Richmond, Virginia as well)
12. Kamala Harris (Attorney General of California)
13. Donna Brazile (Political Strategist)

Business: 1. Sean (P. Diddy) Combs (Founder, Sean John, Bad Boy)
2. Earl G. Graves (Publisher, *Black Enterprise* Magazine)
3. Catherine E. Hughes (Chairperson, Radio One)
4. Magic Johnson (CEO, Magic Johnson Enterprises)
5. Tracy Reese (Fashion Designer and Entrepreneur)
6. David L. Steward (Chairman, World Wide Technology)
7. Carol H. Williams (CEO, Carol H. Williams Advertising)

Religion: 1. Dr. Creflo A. Dollar (Founder and Senior Pastor, World Changers Church International)

2. Minister Louis Farrakhan (Head, Nation of Islam)
3. Bishop T.D. Jakes (Minister, Author, Entrepreneur)
4. Fredrick K. C. Price (Pastor, Crenshaw Christian Center)
5. Janice Willis (Ph.D., Buddhist Scholar)

Arts & Entertainment: 1. Mara Brock Akil (Creator and Executive Producer of "Girlfriends" and other Television Shows)
2. Halle Berry (Academy Award-winning Actress, Producer)
3. Dr. William (Bill) Cosby, Jr. (Comedian, Actor, Producer)
4. Lee Daniels (Filmmaker, Academy Award-nominated Director)
5. Suzanne de Passe (Co-Chair, de Passe Jones Entertainment Group)
6. Quincy Jones (Musician, Producer, Entertainment Executive)
7. Stan Lathan (Producer and director)
8. Spike Lee (Filmmaker, 40 Acres and a Mule Filmworks)
9. Wynton Marsalis (Trumpeter, Composer, Artistic Director of Jazz at Lincoln Center)
10. (Dana Owens) Queen Latifah (Actress, Entertainer, Entrepreneur, Philanthropist)
11. Tyler Perry (Playwright, Author, Director, Producer, Actor)
12. Antonio (LA.) Reid (Chairman, Island Def Jam Music Group, and Producer)
13. Shonda Rhimes (Creator, Writer, and Executive Producer, "Grey's Anatomy")
14. John Singleton (Film Director and Screenwriter)
15. Tavis Smiley (Author, Activist, and Media Personality)
16. Will Smith (Film Actor, Producer, Recording Artist)
17. Denzel Washington (Academy Award-winning Actor, Director, Producer)
18. Oprah Winfrey (Talk Show Host, Entertainment Executive, Actress, and Philanthropist)

Education: 1. Dr. Maya Angelou (Poet, Professor, Actress, Composer, and Author)
2. Lerone Bennett, Jr. (Author, Historian, Lecturer, and *Ebony Magazine* Executive Editor Emeritus)
3. Dr. Michael Eric Dyson (Scholar, Author, and Avalon

Foundation Professor in the Humanities and African American and Religious Studies, University of Pennsylvania)

4. Dr. John Hope Franklin (Historian and James B. Duke Professor Emeritus of History, Duke University; now deceased)

5. Dr. Henry Louis (Skip) Gates, Jr. (W.E.B. Du Bois Professor of the Humanities and Director of the W.E.B. Du Bois Institute for African and African American Research at Harvard University, Author, and Historian)

6. Charles Ogletree (Law Professor, Founding Executive Director of Harvard Law School's Charles Hamilton Houston Institute for Race and Justice)

7. Dr. Cornel West (Author, Scholar, Professor of Religion at Princeton University)

Public Service: 1. Julian Bond (Chairman, NAACP Board of Directors)

2. Rev. Dr. Calvin O. Butts (Educator and Pastor of Abyssinian Baptist Church)

4. Danny Glover (Actor, Activist)

5. Dorothy I. Height (President Emerita for Life, National Council of Negro Women); she is deceased)

6. Rev. Jesse L. Jackson, Sr. (President Rainbow/PUSH Coalition and Civil Rights Activist)

7. Wyclef Jean (Musician, Advocate for Haiti, Founder, Yele Haiti Foundation)

8. Rev. Al Sharpton (Civil Rights Activist and Founder, National Action Network)

This list is very informative, especially for those Black Americans who may need to be made aware of their strength and importance to American culture. The people on this list are very innovative and know how to survive in a hostile, racist society. Blacks bring honor, hope, and respect to the United States. America uses their achievements to legitimize its foreign policy, especially with African and Arab countries. This list proves how strong and intelligent Black Americans are and is proof against the racially-biased reporting about Black intelligence.

49

Whites also have alarming high school dropout rates and commit more crimes in America statistically compared to Blacks. White crimes are not exposed as much by the racist media as Black crimes are.

Blacks are also great organizers. Here is a list of a few of these Organizational Leaders:
1.   Dr. Lezil Baskerville (President & CEO, National Association for Equal Opportunity in Higher Education)
2.   Albert E. Dotson, Jr. (Chairman, 100 Black Men of America, Inc.)
3.   Marian Wright Edelman (President, Children's Defense Fund)
4.   Nicole Lee (Executive Director, TransAfrica Forum)
5.   Alfonso E. Lenhardt (President and CEO, National Crime Prevention Council)
6.   Dr. Betty Davis Lewis (President, National Black Nurses Association)
7.   Dr. Michael L. Lomax (President & CEO, United Negro College Fund)
8.   William Lucy (President, Coalition of Black Trade Unions)
9.   John B. Smith (President, National Newspaper Publishers Association)
10. Peola Smith-Smith (President, National Association of Negro Business & Professional Women's Clubs, Inc.)
11. Calvin Smyre (President, National Black Caucus of State Legislators)
12. Johnny C. Taylor, Jr. (President & CEO, Thurgood Marshall College Fund)
13. Barbara L. Thomas (President and CEO, National Black MBA Association) There are many Black leaders that are not on this list.

Problems for Blacks to Overcome

Problems for Blacks to Overcome

The following are some problems Blacks need to overcome to help insure unity and cooperation with each other: The racial divide is one of the major problems facing Americans. Some of these problems include greed, politician selfishness, unequal justice, political favoritism towards a certain group, lies, deceit and propaganda, etc. These are problems that should be of concern for all Americans and recognized as important issues which need to be discussed. I am sure there are problems that also exist in many other countries. I will address problems in the United States pertaining to particular issues which are of concern to Blacks and all other Americans that are in a state of despair from persecution and racial injustice.

Incidences that I believe are a condition of despair may not be accepted as a condition of despair by others. Some may feel desperate conditions are for their benefit and glory. Here is an example: Blacks believe the holocaust of slavery was their despair. Racist Whites feel it was glory for them. I am using these terms in a general way to convey my point to restore strong pride in Black Americans and their history.

Another problem that is overlooked is the fact that Black Americans are placing their children in the hands of a racist society to be educated by that society. This racist society's criterion is to glorify European culture and achievements while degrading African culture and achievements. Black Americans should unite to take charge of the education of their children and teach them about books and writings of African historical scholars who have written about ordeals and achievements of the

African race. If that happens, I guarantee you will see Black children making great strides in educational achievement. Teaching Black children and adult Blacks about Black historical achievements will make them proud of their race. I will discuss many issues and problems American Blacks are facing. They have survived many horrific situations in the past. Many times their problems have challenged them in unity, strength, courage, and perseverance. Many times their survival depended upon their unity to overcome many barriers placed before them. They are now faced with ordeals and problems that they alone must solve. They are not in the position to blame others for their circumstances; it is in their hands to triumph over adversity as they have successfully done in the past.

The American Black anthem during the Civil Rights struggle was "We Shall Overcome." Blacks are the ones who can rid themselves of the racists' mind control propaganda against them. Another problem that this society keeps hidden from the public is drug trafficking that is permitted in the United States. Drug trafficking is used to hamper Blacks from unifying and becoming a threat to racist control in America. My reason for that statement is simple: American jails are overflowing with Blacks, a great many of whom are accused of committing drug crimes. America leads the world in the incarceration of its citizens.

There is a flagrantly unfair difference in the charging and sentencing of Whites and Blacks who commit similar drug crimes. For example, Whites will be charged with minor violations of drug crimes and even excused with allegations of prescription drug overdose. Sentences for Whites are short jail time and rehab treatments. Blacks' sentences are long jail time and less rehab treatment. Keeping people in jail is more expensive than investing in their education, yet this unfair sentencing of Blacks continues. Educated people will be influenced to be law abiding and less of a strain on the economy. They will be a benefit and not a hardship to the country.

People with criminal records start with a handicap and also lose their right to vote which is the double whammy put upon them. The United States prison system functions to take away the job opportunities and political power of those with criminal records. Former prisoners are left without any incentives to help them survive after being released from prison. The American prison system plays a major role in promoting Black fatherless homes.

The serious crime problems in Black areas must be overcome by community organizations and volunteer patrols of their neighborhoods. It would be helpful for church groups to furnish concerned members to assist in community patrols. Wealthy Blacks should form a unified committee to build or rent buildings to educate their children in true history, science, geography, math, and African religions that have included original involvements of the Black race. Blacks need to be given the opportunity to build pride in their accomplishment of success in receiving educational degrees by working in cooperation to improve their communities, families, and lives. Sports and the arts of dancing, singing, acting, comedy, and music are all important disciplines and those who succeed in them belong to worthy occupations. However, it is also very necessary and important to obtain intelligence and common sense with a loving tolerance of all humanity with understanding of faith, strength, and courage to bring true joy, peace, and happiness into your life. White media and other influence will encourage Blacks to set their goals to achieve fame and fortune through the entertainment and sports fields alone.

In addition, White society will not encourage or permit Black community patrol without imposing confusion or restrictions that will hamper and discourage the ability for those programs to succeed. Community patrol has a better potential to curtail drug traffic where the police have failed. Under police patrol, drug traffic has usually increased in Black neighborhoods. Public informers to the Police Department of drug trafficking in Black

Neighborhoods end up being assaulted, arrested or murdered. Informers are forced to keep quiet about drug trafficking in their neighborhoods.

Some concerned citizens have organized community involvement to assist police in removing drug sales from their neighborhoods. Unfortunately, some of these concerned citizens have been arrested for assault and even murdered when they have protected themselves from attacks by drug peddlers. There is much bribery and corruption in drug traffic that involves many people in all kinds of positions. There are many concerned and honest police officers. There are also a few in cahoots with permitting drug sales especially in Black neighborhoods. Observe where the media highlights the sales of drugs, and the communities where drug sales are prevalent. The media will highlight Black neighborhoods as being very much involved in permitting drug sales. More Whites are drug addicts. Drug enforcement will not permit illegal drugs to be sold on streets in White neighborhoods that are the only areas where it is strictly enforced.

The laws of this country can be interpreted in any manner to control anyone or any situation that racists fear. There is not a law in this country that cannot be interpreted many different ways. The most flagrant abuse of the law's interpretation was during slavery and segregation and it is continued under integration. There is one legal interpretation used for Blacks and another interpretation used for Whites. The written laws are the same but the excuses for different charges depend on the race of the person charged with a crime. Politicians will always refer to the Constitution written by slave owners as having been written by the "founding fathers." They are the writers of the original Constitution that condoned and supported slavery in America. During the era of slavery in America, "All White Men were created equal."

After the Civil War and the additions of three amendments, the 13th, 14th, and 15th, which freed Blacks from slavery and declared they had equal rights under the Constitution, the statement changed to "All men are created equal." Note that a person selected to become a judge of the Supreme Court will be questioned by Senators about their views on the Constitution and their knowledge of its meaning. These Senators should also elaborate on the humanitarian amendments to the Constitution after the Civil War. As Senators discuss the Constitution of the founding fathers, they should be questioned whether they support the original constitution written by slave owners protecting the institution of slavery, or support the 13th, 14th, and 15th Amendments. The Constitution written by slave owners defending slavery before the Civil War is different from the Constitution with the added Amendments freeing slaves after the Civil War. I believe it is important to know if politicians and judges support the Constitution as it supports slavery or the Constitution which freed slaves.

During the era of American slavery, many Whites referred to poor Whites as "White trash." There were no occupations for them to perform for wages as long as slaves were forced to work without wages or compensation. Poor Whites were hired to search for escaped slaves, be on the look-out for slaves' rebellions and to control slaves. They were also used to punish slaves who resisted the inhuman treatment received from Whites.

The term "White trash" was allowed to disappear from American descriptions of dehumanizing poor White people. "Nigger" was a derogatory word used by Whites to describe Black people. Whites encouraged Black comedians to use that word in their comic entertainment. They hired them to perform their acts on television and stages using that word and publicizing them as America's great comedians. Whites have continued to embrace that word when used by rap entertainers yet have encouraged the derogatory term "White Trash" to disappear from American

55

speech and literature. Blacks should be aware of the psychology Whites use to encourage them to degrade their race.

America also has an interpretation for the "Terrorist Watch List." This is a list the United States Government added Nelson Mandela's name to because anyone uprising against racist apartheid was once considered a terrorist. Nelson Mandela's name and his organization, the African National Congress (ANC), were finally removed from that list on June 27, 2008 (just weeks before his 90th birthday).

The U.S. senators said having Mandela on such a list was an "embarrassment" to the United States. The House of Representatives had passed the same legislation on May 8th. Congresswoman Barbara Lee, a California Democrat and co-sponsor of the bill, said she was pleased that the House "was taking the right steps to finally right this inexcusable wrong." Barbara Lee added that the legislation introduced during the 1980s while Ronald Reagan was president was "anachronistic" and that men and women who are heroes and freedom fighters were "wrongfully labeled" as terrorists.

Laws are also different for people who are politicians, government employees, CEOs, wealthy people, etc. Is there equal and fair justice in America? There is no perfect country or society. My only concern is how America breaks down fear and mistrust and misinterprets unity and equality for all.

The best defense against illegal drugs entering the country is to stop smugglers from bringing it into the country. Major defenses to control drug traffic are to arrest the drug smugglers. Drug smugglers have certain ways to successfully bring drugs into the country. It is known but not discussed in the media that drug dealers use bribery and conceal drugs in legal shipping containers, etc., to get illegal drugs into the country. Drug smugglers sell their shipments to drug dealers. Drug dealers hire drug peddlers to sell their drugs on the street. Drug peddlers will use drug addicts, people with criminal records, and people that will not be hired for any honest jobs. These are the people used to peddle drugs on the street. This is one of the reasons that U.S. prisons have so many occupants.

Information about who the drug smugglers are could be obtained from the drug dealers when they are arrested. Information about the drug dealers could be obtained from the drug peddlers when they are arrested. Information about the drug peddlers could be obtained from the low-level drug pushers who mostly already have criminal records when they are arrested. Law enforcement officers will give the excuse that drug felons will not talk for fear of retaliation by organized drug criminals. That will be their excuse for why drug traffic continues to flood the Black community.

Law enforcement officials claim they are able to stop terrorists by all methods necessary or stop many other crimes that threaten the life and safety of the White community. However, when it involves illegal drugs, they have many excuses why it is not stopped or contained and turned into a minuscule problem. Blacks do not have the network to export large quantities of drugs into the country. If drug exporters and suppliers were arrested with the same enthusiasm as Blacks are arrested for buying drugs, our prison population would decrease dramatically. American society divides people into certain categories, giving them labels such as: the Chinese are known for Chinese restaurants, Italians are known for Pizza restaurants, French are known for being great chefs, Whites are known for hard work and getting ahead, etc., yet Blacks are known for (you guessed it) drugs, crime, and school dropouts. The sad part about those negative portrayals is that many people including many Blacks accept this propaganda. Many Black rappers espoused those portrayals of Black society in their rap songs. Black comedians also espoused those negative portrayals in their comedy skits.

There is a Bible quote in Proverbs 18:21 which states, "Death and life are in the power of the tongue." As you speak negative words about yourself, your family, women, or your race, those are your thoughts and your thoughts are you. As you constantly repeat your thoughts, you will surely believe your thoughts are true. On the other side, if you constantly repeat positive thoughts, ideas and respect for women, you will believe in what you say. Positive words encourage positive thinking and will encourage all who hear your positive raps and comedy skits without degrading your women or your race. You will benefit from positive words and thinking and these attitudes and outlook will defeat the racists' propaganda. It will have the potential to bring unity and cooperation within the Black race again.

White racists fear Black unity more than they feared Osama Bin Laden or other terrorists. Another problem and I know this is a touchy subject, is religion. I am a believer in the Almighty and I respect all religious beliefs. I will not impose my beliefs on anyone or let others impose their beliefs on me; I was raised as a Christian. The Black church has been a haven of encouragement and strength for Black people going back to the era of suffering under the holocaust of slavery. We are now in the twenty-first century; we need to have new leadership and direction in achieving equality. We continue to need preachers but, in this new day and time, we need leaders. Blacks need leaders that will not only preach but will lead the people to the promise land. Black ministers should unify with all other religious leaders that believe in freedom and equality regardless of faith, religion or size of the church or congregation.

This life and death struggle continues to this day. The Jena Six incidents in Louisiana should be a wake-up call to prove how bad things are -- and it is getting worse. New civil rights battles have to be fought with renewed criteria and direction, and with dedicated leaders that have the ability to bring unity and direction within the Black race. It is regrettable that some of those in power have used religion to influence people they govern to protect their power and greed. Most humans have spiritual beliefs and awareness of a supreme power. It is unfortunate that some people that have power use the doctrines of different religions to cause conflicts and mayhem towards others. Religion is a centuries-old tradition with many different faiths and beliefs. Is it possible, as centuries have passed, that interpretations of some ancient events as being of a divine nature have been made in order to change the wordings of some biblical writings like the European King James Version of the Bible? Unfortunately, some who claimed to be avid religious believers have committed horrible crimes against humanity. The crime of slavery in the United States was most horrific. The sea voyage of slaves in ships was so horrendous that many jumped overboard to be eaten by sharks in order to escape the hell of slavery. Wall Street in New York City got its name from a wall that was built to block slaves from fleeing the slave markets and jumping into the ocean to drown themselves rather than be sold as slaves. I know in this day and time it is hard to imagine anyone being forced into a similar situation of despair and hopelessness.

Yet, what has happened in the past can happen again in the future.

All my life I have believed in questioning things that I do not understand. I believe anything you do not understand gives you the right as a human being to inquire about it and get other opinions. You learn from observation, interest, knowledge, understanding, and common sense. I will add spiritual awareness, faith and believing in yourself, and consulting with your own spirit through your devoted beliefs for guidance and direction. The majority of humans rely on their faith and beliefs for their courage and strength. I certainly rely on my faith and beliefs. The Christian religion teaches the gospel of Jesus Christ. Much of the world's human population believes in the religion of Christ. Christians often preach that non-believers will die and go to Hell. According to Christian beliefs, much of the world's population that does not believe in the Christian faith is heading to Hell and damnation. I do not know the doctrines of other religions. I am sure their beliefs and religious teachings are somewhat different from the Christians. Christians believe their religion is correct and other religions believe theirs is correct also. Religion is one of the great dividers among humans and sometimes it causes deadly conflicts between them.

Some religions forbid association and fellowship with non-believers of their particular faith or religion. There are some religious faiths in this country that break down the wall of religious divide and will unify people. I personally believe removing religious barriers will encourage humans to communicate and have a better feel for each other, lessening the tendency to have an excuse to commit violent acts upon each other with religious interpretation as the reason for violence.

I will paraphrase an e-mail received from an organization of writers of which I was a member. The e-mail was not sent to me directly. I presumed the author wanted this e-mail to be known and I found it appropriate for my book. This e-mail is a response to an insulting remark about then Senator Barack Obama. I am sharing this e-mail because it is pertinent to my writings about race and religion. E-Mail Paraphrase: The author asks to share his opinion with the readers about an insulting remark to then Senator Barack Obama. His questions are, "Why do we pledge allegiance to the flag?" and "Does this country stand for what it says?" His defense of President Obama when he was accused by some of faithlessness for not using the Holy Bible when being sworn into office was that the Holy Bible has been rewritten over 1,700 times and has been used to oppress people of color (our ancestors). The author states he refuses to allow anyone to call him a Christian, his reason being that he has seen so-called Christians kill people in the name of God.

He calls himself Christ-like and always takes Christ with him every place he goes. He explains he treats everyone, companion, friends, family etc. that he has contact with as though they were Christ Jesus and he respects every soul. He questions whether

60

you love yourself. There also is a challenge for Black folks to think about whether Democrats or Republicans really have done anything for them. The author states his confidence in President Obama to fix issues affecting Black Americans and put America on the right track. He feels confident Blacks will unite and learn their true history to improve their race. His message is, "love yourself and your race and pray for President Barack Obama." Peace and Blessings—TW (End of paraphrase).

Another problem for Blacks is succumbing to the indoctrination of racists in the media and allowing them to portray the African American fight for racial justice and equality with biased views in order to confuse Blacks and stop them from achieving their goals. Here is an example: During the Civil Rights rebellion against injustice and tyranny, Blacks started the movement protesting inequality and unequal justice under the law. Blacks wanted equal treatment and fairness in all things from this society. Many liberal Whites joined Blacks in their struggle. The mainstream media changed Blacks' stated themes for justice and equality for people living under racist unjust laws into a fight for integration only. The media's reporting gave the impression that the goal for Blacks was to sit in a classroom next to a White student. Blacks wanted fair and equal education for their children. They were fighting for equal funding for all schools and the right to enter schools in or close to their neighborhoods.

Blacks were given integration which is a partial achievement of their stated goals for freedom and equality. The racists had hoped this would calm Blacks' anger and divert them from their main goal of fighting for equality and justice in the judicial system. In the future, Blacks should guard against the media changing their words, goals, or direction in their fight against injustice and inequality. This brings me to the next problem, which is linking gay rights to Black struggles against racial injustice. That problem is the burdening of the fight for racial injustice with gay rights issues. This issue is manipulated with the conspiracy of the racists in control and the mainstream

61

media. The media is used to spread confusion among the public because they know the majority of the public will be distasteful about gay rights issues. The media viciously portray Black civil rights issues with gay rights issues in order to have an excuse for no progress in Black civil rights being achieved. You will find in many large bookstores and libraries information pertaining to Black interest, issues, or achievements will be integrated with gay rights books and gay rights issues in the same sections. Racists want to instill the impression that Black issues and gay rights issues are unified causes.

The main purpose of the mainstream media is to influence your approval or disapproval of government programs and policies that are questionable. The media also paint a picture in your mind of the greatness and virtue of American society compared to the supposedly unethical and corrupt conditions of foreign countries. Africa is mostly singled out by the media as mainly an ungovernable continent. America continues to be infected with racist problems of all kinds which mostly affect Black people. America has a large population of Black citizens; I also believe the total number of Black citizens in America is not accurately reported. Some Blacks will pass themselves off as White or another race in order to receive better job opportunities or advantages. The downgrading of Black achievements is not only portrayed in the mainstream media, it is also in American history. This is a picture painted of Blacks regardless of whether they are African American or continental Africans. Racist Americans know the majority of Blacks are intelligent, assertive, strong, creative, etc. Right-wing racists will paint a degrading picture of Blacks to influence people into thinking that Blacks are not capable of governing a country or people. They will paint a glorified picture of American White rule, yet under White rule, there was slavery, lynching, segregation, injustice, etc., along with greed, lies, and corruptions. Another picture of Black portrayal in the American media is too many Black children being raised in fatherless homes.

Fatherless homes are not only a Black problem; there are many fatherless homes that are White also. The media only highlights this as a Black problem. What is not known by Blacks and Whites is the participation of a racist society in that problem. There are many thousands of Black men incarcerated in prisons, and some are fathers who were convicted by racist laws and courts. Not all Blacks are innocent and not all Blacks are guilty either. I do not have to remind anyone of the racist injustices Blacks have suffered under the laws of this country. Blacks convicted of a felony lose their rights to vote, lose their citizenship. When Blacks are convicted and have a criminal record, it is almost impossible to be employed by anyone. After serving time for a felony and being released from behind bars, their future success or life improvement is a big challenge. Some challenges facing them are losing their right to vote, a criminal record being an employment handicap; perhaps their education was interrupted or halted as well. Many things could happen to or influence a person faced with those problems which could result in something good or bad.

Those are the situations that cause many homes and families to break up. Those are major problems the Black race as a whole should address. Unfortunately, some Blacks and Whites are influenced by the negative propaganda espoused by the mainstream media and biased information that is degrading to Blacks. Blacks are not perfect and Whites are not perfect either. Whites have serious crime and drug issues comparable to Black crime issues. Whites also suffer high murder rates among themselves, yet we hear much more about "Black-on-Black" than "White-on-White" crime. Crime is an issue prevalent in the United States that affects the whole population. The media will have you believe it is mainly a Black American issue. That alone should make you aware of what this system is about when it puts all the blame for crime in the United States on Black citizens. The prevalence of crime by all races should be an American issue and not just a Black issue. I am singling out only the racists that are in control of America.

63

There are many liberal Whites who believe in racial equality for all citizens; unfortunately, they are not in power. The mainstream media have succeeded in making some liberal-minded Whites fearful of Black people. The media purposely highlight Blacks committing criminal activities with great intensity. The media will report White criminal activity with less intensity as if it were a rare occurrence. They have also succeeded in making Blacks fearful of other Blacks by the manner in which they report criminal actions. All through American history, Whites have been violent towards themselves as well as towards Blacks. White crimes are prevalent in their neighborhoods as much as Black crime is in their neighborhoods. Crime and violence knows no race difference, yet the mainstream media in the United States highlights Black violence more than White violence. More Blacks are in prison because of racial injustice administered by an unequal judicial system. This system leaves no opportunity for Blacks to be rehabilitated with the same opportunities that are presented to Whites. There are other profound existing problems facing American Blacks that are not discussed or even mentioned by the media. Those problems are racism, lynch law, and gerrymandered voting districts which have the effect of controlling Black votes and assuring White majority rule, etc.

During slavery, whenever a Black man started ordering other Blacks around in a violent or harsh manner, their response to that person would be, "You are acting White." That was the phrase for any incident of being harshly ordered to do some kind of labor by one Black to another. White racists have expanded on that phrase to include success in achieving good grades in schools by Black students. That phrase, "you are acting White," according to the White racist is to brainwash African Americans to mean if you achieve good grades, you are accomplishing what White students are capable of doing. This is a sinister purpose by White racists and that is to belittle African American achievements while encouraging disputes among them about getting good grades and working hard in school. This is to give

64

students with poor grades more reasons to be resentful and not to achieve in school. Racists will interpret any sayings or laws to cause distrust, arguments, or disunity among Blacks. There are no intelligent Blacks that believe working hard to achieve an excellent education is "acting White." Blacks do not believe education is a Whites-only goal. That phrase pertaining to Blacks working hard to achieve good grades in schools has been planted by racist Whites in order for them to reap the harvest of causing resentment between Blacks who are achievers and Blacks that failed to achieve good grades. There are Blacks that have used that phrase in jest and resentment. When that phrase has been used in resentment against other Black achievers, a point has been scored by racists in their quest to plant the conception that you should be White and not Black to succeed in school.

Throughout American history, propaganda was created to identify being White with likeability, success, intelligence and good conduct. American propaganda continued portraying Blacks as ugly, failures, unintelligent, and people with bad behavior. They have not exposed their violations of inhuman treatment, forced segregation, forced education of historical lies, and the injustices which Blacks have had to resist in order to survive.

Black Inventors and Achievements

Black Inventors and Achievements

The following is a list of some Black inventors and their inventions:

1. Patricia Bath: developed the Cataract Laserphaco Probe.

2. Andrew Beard: received a patent for a device he called the Jenny Coupler. The Jenny Coupler automatically joined cars by simply allowing them to bump into each other, or as Beard described it, the "horizontal jaws engage each other to connect the cars".

3. Otis Boykin: invented an improved electrical resistor used in computers - radios - television sets and a variety of electronic devices. Boykin's resistor helped reduce the cost of those products. Otis Boykin also invented a variable resistor used in guided missile parts, a control unit for heart stimulators, a burglar-proof cash register and a chemical air filter.

4. Charles Brooks: of Newark, New Jersey invented improvements to street sweeper trucks that he patented on March 17, 1896. His truck had revolving brushes attached to the front fender and the brushes were interchangeable with scrapers that could be used in winter for snow removal.

5. John Albert Burr: patented improved rotary blade lawn mower. Burr designed a lawn mower with traction wheels and a rotary blade designed to not easily get plugged up from lawn clippings. John Albert Burr also improved the design of lawn mowers by making it possible to mow closer to building and wall edges.

6. Dr. George R. Carruthers: astrophysicist, and an inventor as well, he was instrumental in the design of lunar surface ultraviolet cameras. Image Converter, Radiation Detector.

7. George Washington Carver: an agricultural chemist, Carver discovered three hundred uses for peanuts and hundreds more

uses for soybeans, pecans and sweet potatoes. Among the listed items that he suggested to southern farmers to help them economically were his recipes and improvements to/for: adhesives, axle grease, bleach, buttermilk, chili sauce, fuel briquettes, ink, instant coffee, linoleum, mayonnaise, meat tenderizer, metal polish, paper, plastic, pavement, shaving cream, shoe polish, synthetic rubber, talcum powder and wood stain.

8. Dr. Charles R. Drew: system for the storing of blood plasma (blood bank) revolutionized the medical profession. Dr. Drew also established the American Red Cross blood bank, of which he was the first director, and he organized the world's first blood drive, nicknamed "Blood for Britain."

9. Clatonia J. Dorticus: Photo Print Wash and Photo-Embossing Machine.

10. Meredith Gourdine: He pioneered the research of electrogasdynamics. Electrogasdynamics is a way to disperse fog and smoke. By applying strong electrical forces to either, you can control those elements. He was responsible for the engineering technique termed Incineraid for aiding in the removal of smoke from buildings. His work on gas dispersion developed techniques for dispersing fog from airport runways. He also created a generator that allowed for the cheaper transmission of electricity. He held more than 40 patents for various inventions.

11. Frederick McKinley Jones: He is one of the most prolific Black inventors ever. Frederick Jones patented more than sixty inventions, however, he is best known for inventing an automatic refrigeration system for long-haul trucks in 1935 (a roof-mounted cooling device). Jones was the first person to invent a practical, mechanical refrigeration system for trucks and railroad cars, which eliminated the risk of food spoilage during long-distance shipping trips. The system was, in turn, adapted to a variety of other common carriers, including ships. He also invented a self-starting gas engine and a series of devices for the early film industry, including one for adapting silent movie projectors for talking films, and developing box office

equipment such as a ticket-dispensing machine and another that gave change.

12. W.A. Lavalette: Printing Press.

13.Jan Ernst Matzeliger: Helped to revolutionize the shoe industry by developing a shoe lasting machine that attach the sole to the shoe in one minute.

14.Elijah McCoy: first invention was a lubricator for steam engines, which allowed machines to remain in motion to be oiled; his new oiling device revolutionized the industrial machine industry. His other inventions included an ironing board and lawn sprinkler.

15. Garrett A. Morgan: invention was an early traffic signal that greatly improved safety on American's streets and roadways. Indeed, Morgan's technology was the basic for modern traffic signals and was an early example of what we know today as Intelligent Transportation Systems. He was an inventor and businessman from Cleveland who invented a device called the "Morgan safety hood and smoke protector" in 1914.On July 25, 1916, Garrett Morgan made national news for using his gas mask to rescue 32 men trapped during an explosion in an underground tunnel 250 feet beneath Lake Erie.

16. Alice Parker of Morristown, New Jersey, invented a new and improved gas-heating furnace that provided central heating.

17. Dr. Daniel Hale Williams: credited with having performed open-heart surgery on July 9, 1893 before such surgeries were established. In 1913, Daniel Hale Williams was the only African American member of the American College of Surgeons.

18. Granville T. Woods: developed a system for overhead electric conducting lines for railroads, which aided in the development of the overhead (or elevated) railroad systems found in cities such as Chicago, St. Louis, and New York City. In his early thirties, he became interested in thermal power and steam-driven engines. And, in 1889, he filed his first patent for an improved steam-boiler furnace. In 1892, a complete Electric Railway System was operated at Coney Island, NY. In 1887, he patented the Synchronous Multiplex Railway telegraph which allowed communications between train stations from moving

trains. Granville T. Woods' invention made it possible for trains to communicate with the station and with other trains, so they knew exactly where they were at all times.

There are enormous amounts of inventions by African Americans. I have named a relative few to inform the American people of the great contributions which have helped to make America a powerful nation. More information can be obtained from "Black Inventors A-Z" on this web site: http://inventors.about.com/library/blblackinventors.htm?p=1

These Black inventors are also the ones that brought attention and admiration to America from the world.

Racist Mind Control Methods

Racist Mind Control Methods

Black Americans are the strength and backbone of this nation. Inventions by American Blacks have contributed greatly to the portrayal of America as a prosperous, strong nation. Black Union Army soldiers played a decisive role in defeating the Confederate Army during the Civil War. American Blacks have proven their devotion, loyalty, patriotism, and hope for a better America for all citizens. They have bestowed honor and respect on the United States by excelling in the Olympic Games. With the help and participation of Black athletes, America is usually one of the countries that receives the most gold and silver medals in the Summer Olympics.

Whites have brainwashed Black Americans to believe they must prove themselves to be as good and as smart as they are. Many of the great accomplishments Blacks have achieved for America have been claimed by Whites as theirs so that they could take most of the glory, credit and financial reward. It is time for Blacks to realize they no longer have to prove anything more to anyone. African Americans must remove the brainwashing and realize it is now time for Whites to prove to Blacks that they respect and honor their devotion and loyalty to the United States. It is up to Black leaders to lead a unified Black population to repair those degrading anti-Black images which right-wing racists have deliberately planted in the minds of the American people. A picture of pride and unity will only be achieved when Black historical knowledge is being taught to Blacks by their well-informed scholars.

Another problem I will bring to the forefront is one that could have an obstructive effect on some dedicated, successful Black leaders in terms of their continued struggle for justice and equality for all. First, I will give the background to this problem that will be presented to you. I will start by stating racists in power control the media, economics, judicial system, and law enforcement when it suits their purpose. They also set policies that are to their advantage. Racists are White people who believe in White control and privileges over all other non-Whites.

There are many Whites who are liberal-minded and believe in equality for all races. Racist Whites believe liberal Whites are, as they would be called in the old days, "nigger lovers." In this modern day and time, you can hear the hateful language directed towards liberal Whites by the racists who control mainstream media. The media plays an important role in promoting White control while portraying Black control in a negative light. The information you hear, read, or observe influences your beliefs, thoughts, and actions. I will present information on this subject in my summary of this section.

The problems Blacks have in this country are serious ones that the whole country should be concerned. There is a saying, "a house divided cannot stand." There is no logical reason why this country cannot be a racially mixed country with equality and justice for all races, including electing government officials that will be represented by more than just the White race.

Racists are the ones that believe in White supremacy, control, and privileges. They believe they are better, smarter, and the most civilized race on earth. They believe all other races are inferior to them. They teach that doctrine to themselves and their children. They also teach this doctrine to the people they once forced into slavery. The White doctrines teach that God has given Whites the right to bring civilization to the Black race because Blacks are uncivilized heathens.

Liberal Whites have an opposite view. They believe all people are human beings and created equal under God, and they have compassion for the inhuman treatment slaves had to endure. Many have fought for the freedom of enslaved Blacks and their descendants. Unfortunately, they were in the minority.

Historically, right-wing racists have taken advantage of Black women and raped them. Many Black women became pregnant from forced sex by White slave owners and overseers. America is a mixed-race nation. It is likely that many racist Whites have Black blood due to their hidden Black ancestry. There is no pure race in the world. Americans are judged by skin complexion. In America, Blacks can have a light complexion or fair skin and pass for White. A person that believes in Western or European culture is considered to be of the White race. If you are a very fair-skinned Black passing for White and your values are of European culture, you are considered White.

An African American admits their ancestors are from the continent of Africa. If you are fair-skinned, maybe even appear White, yet honor African values and culture that are accepted as your heritage, then you are considered to be an African American. True African Americans are proud of their race, culture, and values and have not been brainwashed. They have their own values, expectations, and interests. They are not selfish and believe in helping and looking out for one another. They believe what happens to one will happen to all. They feel each other's pains. Unfortunately, not all Blacks feel that same kind of pride for their race. Blacks who do not feel pride in the suffering their race endured and in its achievements are selfish and look out for themselves.

Some Blacks are interested in greed and what benefit they can obtain for themselves. They believe in White doctrines and White greed; their goal is to please Whites and keep them in control. They are known as Negroes, sellouts, and House Negroes. They will not unite with other Blacks in struggle for equality, justice, and equal opportunity. Negroes will expose themselves as to whom they are when they insult Black civil

72

rights leaders or talk against pro-Black issues. A Negro will support White issues over Black ones. Negroes will not participate in any civil rights movements. They are brainwashed to believe the holocaust of slavery was an American birth defect only, and not a horrible crime of man's inhumanity to man.

Black leaders who are successful in bringing unity and organization to their race should be aware of right-wing racists' determination to discredit them among their people and the public at large. Here are some methods that are used to dishonor Black leaders. There are many ways this is accomplished. I cannot list all of the ways that are used, but I will list some and let you be the judge of other ways and means used. I will list them numerically in order to be used as reference points.

1. Create mistrust and disunity among different Black groups: The media will put one Black group against the other to keep them from uniting. They will claim a degrading remark was made by one group towards another. They will minimize one group by saying the other group has more support and followers. They will claim one group is not as organized as another is. Whenever a group or leader of a group makes a statement at an interview, the media will take the statement out of context and report it in a damaging manner to incite disagreements among people or groups. Not all groups will be equal in some respects; that is common sense. The main purpose groups must remember is, regardless of their size, they have the same goal in the fight for equality. Regardless of how large or how much support a group receives, a united goal comprising different groups will make them a very large, united organization that will surpass any individual group's movement. United groups are gigantic and powerful.

I have just named a few methods used to create mistrust among Black groups. There are many more. One more tactic used by the racists to thwart Black unity is that they will plant spies and disrupters in Black groups. Disrupters are Negroes and phony

White liberals. They are used to spread lies, confusion, and mistrust within and among groups in order to get them to argue or fight with each other. There could be forty or more Black men and women united for a cause working in cooperation with one another. It will take no more than one or two of the wrong type of persons to get involved with Black groups to cause disunity, arguments, and turmoil between them and hamper their attempts at reaching their goals. This type of racist person will have a friendly conversation with a group member about a person's statement heard or was disclosed to him. He will then repeat the conversation with distortions to others in a manner that will cause resentment against certain people or groups.

2. Instigate religious suspicion, distrust, and disunity, and encourage religious hatred between groups: Racists will use religion to discourage unity among the different Black groups. They will claim certain religions are teaching their subjects to hate your religious beliefs. Take note: when you are taught to think that way about different religions, your religion is also teaching you to hate other religious beliefs and to fear that religion. When you are not careful, others will use religion as an excuse to cause havoc. People may confuse religion with spiritual convictions, feelings, and beliefs that the Creator has given us, such as a love for all people. We are all human beings basically wanting and searching for the same human qualities of peace, love, joy, happiness, and blessings for all. Religions are a belief system of certain rituals, rites, denominations, etc.

Most of humanity believes in a Creator of this world and applies special beliefs to particular doctrines. Many of these special beliefs are broken down into different religious denominations. Some religious denominations will differ because of the dispersals of the human race on the face of the globe. Religions of different beliefs sometimes cause disputes and problems between humans. Many problems would be curtailed if it were possible for humans to respect each other's religions and not impose their beliefs on others by force or intimidation.

Converting others peacefully to a particular religion with love, patience, understanding, and compassion will help to cut down resentment against certain religious groups. I want it understood, I am not making any accusations against any religion, and I am speaking about religions in a general way.

3. Hint at or accuse successful leaders of criminal acts:
Racists will also use the mainstream media to accuse a Black leader of some act of impropriety. Their goal is to place doubts or suspicions on a Black leader regardless of whether the accusations are true or not. Charges of any sort force these leaders and/or their organizations to hire lawyers and incur financial debts to fight such charges. That causes a tremendous financial strain on civil rights organizations. The goal of the racists is to cause financial strain and crush unified resistance.

4. Accuse a person of committing sexual crimes and involvement of drugs: Right-wing racists have a field day when making accusations against Black leaders of possible sex and drug crimes or drug involvement of any sort.

5. Bring up possible tax problems or corruption:
Racists will scrutinize Black organizations of any kind for tax improprieties. They will not hesitate to accuse successful Black organizations of improper business operations.

I will present a paraphrased portion of an article from the *New York Amsterdam News* published Dec. 26, 2007. I am not focusing on the truth or accuracy of the article. My concern is to show examples of tactics that are used by certain officials to harass or curtail activities of civil rights leaders or their organizations. Rev. Sharpton and associates subpoenaed:
(This article was written by Herb Boyd).
Rev. Sharpton and several of his associates and employees were served subpoenas to be questioned about their financial records and possible tax fraud.

The subpoenas were for the purpose of gaining their financial books and records related to the National Action Network to check on the tax filing of Rev. Al and his organization. The federal government served those subpoenas less than a month after Rev. Sharpton led a Washington March demanding federal action in the Jena Six case, being outspoken of what he believes were injustices towards the Black youths. Rev. Sharpton stated he believes this is harassment to curtail his Civil Rights battle for equal justice for Black Americans.
(End of paraphrase).

6. Accuse a person of incidents in the past which may include violations of a law or tax evasion: Racists will go back years in the past to find anything they can accuse popular Black politicians of doing. It has been reported Black politicians have been under investigation by the U.S. Attorney's office for many years with no charges filed against them. Some wondered if U.S. Attorneys were out to harass certain Blacks. These types of activities have been noted as Black officials of the federal, state and local levels have been routinely investigated at disproportionate rates, often only to later be found not guilty. In the process, however, their reputations were stained and some are still viewed as criminals even though they were exonerated.

7. Being charged making statements claimed by the media as false and inaccurate: Mainstream media make many untrue statements about Blacks. However, they are quick to accuse Blacks of making inaccurate statements and charge them with committing criminal acts such as libel against other persons. Racists will charge Blacks and Black organizations with anything that can force them into court and drain their finances in legal battles.

8. Offer influential civil Rights leader's bribery to encourage them to stop their work for Black empowerment:

9. Right-wingers will display Negroes on television supporting right-wing racists' agendas.

10. Right-wingers will promote a Negro to be the head of a particular organization of theirs in order to give the appearance of fairness and equality. It takes Black Americans to participate in certain groups' political disputes to make them appear authentic. For example, if you have an all-White group advocating equality, it will be hard to believe they are sincere. African Americans need to understand the strength and influence they have on American politics.

These are some of the methods used by racist Whites. Regardless of whether there are legitimate reasons for the charges or not, their primary goal is to discredit Black leaders or groups in order to disorganize and discourage them. Racists want all charges to succeed against Black leaders regardless of their actual guilt or innocence. That has always been the history of racists in America. Their goal is to not let Blacks unify with each other or other people. They will search every record or incident they can use to discredit successful leadership. I realize there is a possibility some accusations may have some merit to them. Blacks are not perfect human beings. However, one must also examine the crimes, corruptions, sex violations, immoral acts, etc. committed by White officials overlooked or mitigated as not serious enough for criminal violations. It has been reported in news articles and web sites how government and law officers' tactics were used to set-up victims to be charged with planning or committing crimes. Some entrapments involve planting evidence on a person for a crime, fraud, misconduct, or sexual improprieties. The following is in substance to the practice of instituting entrapments of a person. Be aware, all entrapment situations are variable and used at the discretion of political and racial groups in power. These tactics are mostly used against Blacks, particularly if they are influential or powerful.

Some elements that constitute entrapments consist of plans by law officials to use an informer to be a witness against a person charged with conspiring to commit or plan any unlawful act. Officials will either hire an individual or give a felon a choice of working with them in order to receive less jail time or a pardon for a criminal act. With careful selections, they instruct the informer which procedures to follow to set-up the victims.

The informer will become friendly and chummy with groups or individuals to entice them to plan unlawful crimes or actions. Informers may set-up to record illegal plans or actions. Informers will be given supplies or equipment needed to entice victims to operate their criminal acts. This has been charges from victims of entrapment against authorities. This has become a major part of the government's approach in certain cases. Unfortunately, these tactics of entrapment are used many times against Blacks. They must be alert to the many different tricks and schemes the racists will play to discredit them. Unfortunately, racists control the judicial system, and that is the process that puts Black people's lives and freedom in jeopardy. This unfair treatment of Blacks was shown by the judicial system's charges of crimes committed by the "Jena 6" Black students while no charges were filed against White students pertaining to the same incident. When Black women are raped, tortured, or murdered by Whites, there is no national news or media coverage. There was a *New York Amsterdam News* article of a young Black groom in New York City killed by police on the eve of his wedding day. Many Black teenagers face more jail time for an altercation with a school official than Whites do. A young Black male teenager will face long jail time for having consensual sex with a teenage White girl.

The following information is paraphrased from a web page which, unfortunately, is no longer available:
http://www6.comcast.net/news/articles/national/2007/10/31/Katrina.Bridge.Blockade/
Hurricane Katrina was an unprecedented American catastrophe.

The following is another aspect of the disaster the media will not cover or discuss in a public forum. Several thousand Black people were stranded at the New Orleans Convention Center without food or water. They were told to cross the Mississippi River Bridge to be evacuated from the city of New Orleans. Police from Suburban Gretna blocked them as they tried to flee New Orleans on September 1, 2007, three days after the storm hit. When the evacuees did not stop, the police fired warning shots in their direction. The Americans trying to flee from a disaster were stopped from reaching safety and getting help by uniformed American police officers. This town did not send food, water or aid of any sort. They did not want their town crowded with a multitude of Blacks. Can you imagine a future America where there is turmoil, and towns or communities have to relocate for their safety in this racist society?

The case raised widespread allegations of racism and a grand jury will not charge anyone in the police blockade that stopped people from escaping that disastrous situation. This is proof that some American communities will not receive other Americans with open arms in love and concern for their well-being. Mainstream media will degrade affirmative action by stating that unqualified Blacks are given jobs or educational opportunities to meet racial quotas. The media will not report that unqualified Whites are given opportunities or jobs because of political connections or because of their wealthy family's donations to a politician or college. Some colleges will pass some failing Whites in order to have their donations increased in the future. Whites do not need affirmative action because unqualified Whites will always receive job opportunities over qualified Blacks. That has been proven to be the case throughout the history of this country. Belonging to the White race is the guaranteed affirmative action reward.

The following is paraphrased, in part, from an article taken from *The Baltimore Afro-American* newspaper, dated September 29, 2007 – October 5, 2007. This article was a commentary by Dr.

Henrie Treadwell. The suppression of Black votes has been accomplished in modern-day America by disenfranchising prisoners and former convicts. In too many states, ex-convicts have returned to society to find that they have been punished again with the lash of disenfranchisement. America's inmate population has exploded, and so has the proportion of incarcerated African Americans. As Blacks make up half of the nation's prison population (though less than 12 percent of the general public), the disenfranchisement of felons is a de facto suppression of Black votes, like the poll tax in the Jim Crow era.

Not surprisingly, a great number of disenfranchised ex-convicts live in four southern states: Alabama, Florida, Kentucky, and Virginia. Nearly 1.5 million people are prevented from voting in those states. When the presidential election of 2000 was decided by Supreme Court intervention after a likely vote-counting error involving less than 100,000 Florida votes, it became painfully clear how not counting or undercounting votes is an injustice. What can be said of preventing people from voting who have paid their debt to society?

Today, roughly six million people cannot vote because of state laws restricting the voting rights of former convicts. Dr. Treadwell advises, "Most other Western democracies have national voting standards, rather than leaving it to states or provinces; other countries also do not restrict voting for men and women who have served prison time." Yet, the U.S. is turning back the clock to a time when only a privileged few were allowed to vote. As the nation's prison population raises, Dr. Treadwell notes, "there are 35 states prohibiting felons from voting while they are on parole; 30 states preventing felony probationers from voting; and 14 states precluding former felons who have completed their sentence from voting." He adds that, "several [southern] states have revised their constitutions and criminal codes to target minorities by linking voting restrictions to crimes committed predominantly by Blacks." He also correctly urges that this "blatant discrimination against Blacks should not be allowed to persist, and it will fall upon our communities to push state governments to correct this grave wrong;" and this author agrees. (End of paraphrased commentary from Dr. Henrie Treadwell).

Americans should recognize the United States' new version of segregation in this modern, post-2000 era. The old ways of lynch mobs and Jim Crow are too obvious to be continued in these times. Racists realize it would be too dangerous for the country to survive under those past horrific conditions. Blacks today are more forceful and determined not to return to the old days of slavery, segregation, and lynching. Blacks have removed the chains from their wrists and their ankles. They have one more chain to remove; it is the mind control chain. When they remove that chain from their minds and free themselves, they will also free Whites from their misguided teachings of White supremacy.

Blacks must really look at themselves and see who they really are and not see or believe what a racist society said they are. Years of slavery, years of brainwashing, and years of social conditioning to accept inferiority have taken their toll on Black American humanity. It is their responsibility to regain their greatness. They do not need the approval of others; they only need the approval of themselves. When Blacks receive the mindset that they should honor their race and themselves then the chains of racist mind control will be removed and they will be able to shout as Dr. King once did, "Free at last, Free at last, Thank God Almighty, we are free at last!"

There are too many injustices to Black American citizens to write about. Injustices to Blacks in this country date back centuries. Time for a change is way, way over due. Changes will only occur with Black unity and their determination for it to become true. Black Americans have made America a great country with the cooperation of liberal Whites in promoting unity, freedom, and equality for all. Right-wing racists are using unequal legal systems to keep Blacks under their control.

They try to hide their racist undercover actions through the unjust legal system that has one set of punishments for Blacks and another for Whites. Whites are often sentenced as though they committed white-collar crimes while Blacks are often sentenced as though theirs were serious criminal actions. It seems Blacks have integrated into a burning house.

The Ku Klux Klan is alive and still active. Today they are smarter and wiser. They have the intelligence to know that in order to continue their racist activities; they will have to be disguised. They hide their racist activities under the cloak of religion and social causes. They no longer call themselves the Ku Klux Klan; their new names are the Religious Right, the Right Wing, Evangelicals, the Aryan Nation, Birthers, etc.

There are some racists in the Republican Party, Democratic Party, and the Independent Party. Their philosophy is White rule and White privileges. They are included in the judicial system, the government, district attorney's offices, and police forces. Racists also control the media and the educational curriculum in schools. Their philosophy is to build up White intelligence and downplay Black intelligence. It is important for Black Americans and all Americans to be aware of racial lynching that is being used under the disguise of legality under law.

I will now use excerpts from a very relevant article and add my own observations. The newspaper article was written by Lamont Muhammad in the *New York Amsterdam News* dated February 18, 2009 and its title was, "Another Mumia Abu-Jamal?" The article is about Brian Tyson, 49, who is a journalist, photographer, radio announcer, actor, amateur boxer, entrepreneur, and graduate of Baltimore's Morgan State University. He bought a home in Philadelphia for his family. A violent drug gang started selling crack cocaine, angel dust, and heroin from an abandoned building near his home.

When Tyson realized what was going on, he informed the local police of this activity. He also organized his neighbors to shut the spot down. Those in Black neighborhoods know that when you report drug activities to the police, drug gangs will retaliate against you. In order for drug gangs to retaliate against an informer, they have to know who the informer is. Tyson's home and vehicle were sprayed with shotgun blasts. He contacted the local police and led them to the house the gang used to sell drugs. The police found Damon "Debo" Miller and the sawed-off shotgun that was used to spray Tyson's home and vehicle earlier. The shotgun was confiscated. No arrest was made. Tyson agreed to testify at a trial that was set for Sept. 24, 1997.

The night before the trial, as Tyson was preparing his vehicle, he smelled a strong scent of gasoline. Suddenly he was struck on his back, he ran to escape the apparent danger. He later testified in court that he heard a shot and returned fire with his legally registered handgun at two men he saw with guns. When the smoke cleared, the same Mr. Miller he and the police found at the street crack house back in February lay dead. He had a warm pistol in his waist and a bundle of crack tucked in his rectum, according to reports. Police also found an empty gasoline container behind Tyson's home where his vehicle had been doused with gasoline. Tyson was convicted [under the lynch law] for third-degree murder in December 2000. He is currently serving a 10-30 year prison sentence in Bellefonte, PA.

"If Tyson had been White, he'd be a celebrated hero and the subject of a Disney movie," wrote syndicated columnist and attorney Lloyd "Kam" Williams. Little was known of the case outside of Philadelphia. But during a radio interview on New York's WBAI-FM last year, Williams described Tyson as another Mumia Abu-Jamal. One of Tyson's neighbors agreed. He testified in a recent affidavit that Tyson was a good neighbor whom the police targeted for attempting to disrupt the open-air drug market near his home.

Alvin Feagins, a neighbor of Tyson, wanted to testify at the trial in defense of Tyson. Alvin and his family were frightened off by city officials. Feagins stated in his affidavit, the Philadelphia Police Department or District Attorney's office visited his home a few days after the shoot-out, and asked his father and family if they knew Mr. Tyson. He continued, "They told us Tyson sold drugs and they found a lot of money and guns in his house." His family was told, "It would not be in our best interest or the interest of the neighborhood if any member of your family testified as a witness for Tyson or got involved in any way." These remarks were stated in Feagins' affidavit. Tyson has submitted that affidavit to the court. Another neighbor, Christine Saunders, agreed with Tyson's self-defense claim. Christine described the neighborhood to the *Philadelphia Inquirer* as an armed camp. Christine and her husband decided to move when a bullet shattered their front window and the police attempted to arrest her husband for reporting the incident. This was her statement to the paper.

Beginning in 2001, Tyson's appeals have fallen on deaf ears in this state. The U.S. Court of Appeals for the third circuit agreed with Tyson's argument. They granted his pro se application for a certificate of appeal in 2007. He has been writing and filing his own briefs since, and awaits decision. This case has focused attention on whether judges and district attorneys are upholding the law, or functioning as agents of chaos, loss and death for a certain population in neighborhoods like Tyson's. Brian Tyson has been fighting for fair and equal justice behind bars for nearly a decade. He is a Black educated citizen concerned for his community and family. Brian Tyson's concern for his community prompted him to organize other concerned community residents to rid the community of illegal drug traffic through informing the police of drug activity in their community. (End of Tyson story excerpts).

The following information of a concerned citizen reporting to the police about drug activity in their neighborhood is a subject I wrote about in my first book, "SSID---- Slavery, Segregation, Integration, Degradation." I will present this writing in its entirety. This subject is in line with citizens informing police of drug activity and protection for or against police informers. This is information about the Dawson family living in Baltimore, Maryland who decided to take a stand against drug trafficking in their neighborhood. Carnell and Angela Dawson, along with their five children, were murdered because they were concerned citizens and were determined to assist the police in eliminating the illegal drug trade in their neighborhood. The police arrested Darrell Brooks, a low-level drug addict, for the murders of the Dawson family. Arresting Darrell Brooks who is an addicted drug user and a known felon that is constantly arrested by the police will not stop or solve the drug trafficking in any neighborhood. His record included armed robbery, assault, theft, and drug possession. He was on probation for a gun charge the night he was charged for setting fire to the Dawson's home. The media reported that he confessed to throwing the firebomb into the Dawson's home because they snitched to the police about drug dealers. Mrs. Dawson had given the police information about drug trafficking in her neighborhood.

I find it very strange that a low-level drug addict on probation would know the name and address of a citizen who had informed the police of illegal drug activity in the neighborhood. This horrible crime brought attention to the neighborhood. The media stated that the police increased patrols, and money was being allocated to drug treatment programs. Baltimore Mayor Martin O'Malley made statements in the *Baltimore Sun* dated August 29, 2003 that the city was giving aid and assistance to the neighborhood. The Mayor continued by stating this fight will continue every day to combat drugs.

According to reports in that same paper, residents continue to complain that the neighborhood looks now as it did on that awful morning in October, 2002, right after the fire in the Dawson's home. Some people in the neighborhood still complained that things are back to normal with continued drug problems.

All the police did was arrest a drug addict with a criminal record who would do anything, commit any crime for a payment of a drug dose when he followed orders from the dealers or suppliers. There were no major crackdowns or major drug busts of suppliers or sellers during that horrific destruction of the precious lives of the Dawson's and their children. What happened with the information the police received from the Dawson's about drugs being sold in their neighborhood? A crime of that magnitude has put fear into the neighborhood, with a warning to others not to go to the police for protection because they may receive catastrophic harm as the Dawson family did.

Black communities have the fear of drugs being sold on their streets while corrupt police inform drug dealers of neighborhood complainants. Police apathy or compliance with drug sales on street corners and in abandoned homes in Black neighborhoods is a legitimate fear for concerned citizens. This fear for honest people to get involved is one of the excuses used by racists to claim Black neighborhoods are bad investments. This excuse permits Black neighborhoods to deteriorate. Crimes that are committed in White neighborhoods will not be exposed as viciously or as widely as the media will expose it in Black neighborhoods. White neighborhoods have their criminals and drug addicts, and they are just as numerous as in Black neighborhoods. This horrendous crime against the Dawson family with the arrest of only one low-level, expendable drug addict is proof to all in the neighborhood that drug suppliers and dealers will not end. Drug dealers and suppliers will entice drug addicts to do their dirty work for them.
This is reminiscent of slavery days when the southern aristocrats paid poor Whites to control Black people forced into slavery.

Drug trafficking is permitted in Black neighborhoods in order to control Blacks and stop them from uniting and organizing. Drug suppliers that hire drug sellers should be arrested and sentenced to prison in order to truly control drug trafficking in Black neighborhoods. Drug suppliers and distributors are controlled by Whites. They are not arrested or incarcerated as prevalently as Black drug buyers are. White drug buyers also are not arrested or incarcerated as much as Black drug buyers are. In Black neighborhoods, the selling of drugs is permitted and encouraged by racists in control. Laws against the sales of drugs in White neighborhoods are more strictly enforced. The drug culture is tied to the control and incarceration of Blacks and is used to camouflage the racism imposed on them. A case in point is the unjust, uneven drug enforcement laws.

Section Two will highlight the cooperation between liberal Whites and African Americans working together for a united America in freedom and equality for all by replacing the racist agenda of dividing Americans by race, religion, etc.

Racist Whites forced Black people during slavery to address all White males regardless of their ages as "Masters," young White unmarried women as "Miss," and older, married White women as "Missy." The word "Master" evolved to another word which sounds similar to it, and that word is "Mister." Mister was used by White males to address each other with respect. The words "Miss" or "Missy" evolved into the words "Miss" for unmarried White girls and "Mrs." for married White women. Racist Whites addressed elderly Black males as "uncle" and those of all other ages as "boy," and elderly Black females as "auntie" while all younger Black females were called "gal." Yet there were horribly severe punishments imposed upon Blacks if racist Whites felt Blacks did not show enough respect to them. They labeled that action as Blacks acting "uppity."

American society has portrayed Blacks living under forced slavery conditions as a happy, carefree people serving White masters with love and loyalty. These lies are produced in motion pictures, untrue American History, and media propaganda. Under American slavery, human beings were denied respect and the right to make their own life decisions, and they were not able to protect their families or have control over meeting their sexual needs. Enslaved people were also forced to watch their children or other loved ones being sold away from them as if they were merchandise.

Regardless of the racist propaganda, there is no joy or happiness of any kind living in a forced slavery life. Any societies or government that condones slavery is a country of savages and should not proclaim to be a country of equality and freedom. Slavery played a major part in defining what America truly was. America was born in slavery and laws were passed by the government condoning and supporting its continuation.

American slave society was the beginning of the mind control of African Blacks and White Americans. For hundreds of years, Blacks and Whites were brainwashed to accept slavery as the natural evolution of civilized Whites. Whites in power claimed they were uplifting Black Africans from a state of savagery. This is the information White American history espouses pertaining to Blacks and Native Americans--that the latter were savages and would attack and kill Whites, while Blacks were cannibals that would eat human flesh. It is hard to believe any of this now, but that is what I read and heard through the media, movies, and history books during my school-age years.

It is now an emergency like no other for African Americans to free themselves of mind control from a racist American society. They have to begin by teaching themselves true history. Once Blacks learn true history, that is when they will realize the jealousy and resentment the Europeans had for the greatness of the Black Race. Black History will force great respect and pride to return within Blacks so that they will educate the world about the greatness of their ancestors. When Black Americans control the education of their race and teach true history, it will also benefit White Americans because they will better understand how all Americans have contributed towards making America a great country.

The following web site is informative:
http://www.maxpages.com/seminar/blackhistory
The section I will paraphrase is called "The Truth about Black History" and it was written by Melvin F. Miller. This is a quote from Melvin F. Miller: "Learning more about the true facts and events of history can help us to better understand where we came from and where we must go to solve our problems."
Paraphrase: In ancient times, the lands of the black and brown people were the central gathering place for the entire world. Africa, the Land of the Blacks, had become a wonderful and highly developed spiritual land. The wonders of the Pyramids of Egypt is still a mystery to the modern world. Africa was the cradle of civilization where humans first created organized ways of living. Greeks, other Europeans, and other people of the world learned from Africans about arts, science, herbal medicine, architecture, mathematics, astrology, and spirituality.

American school textbooks have perpetrated negative stereotypes of Africa and Black people. American schools' curriculum is filled with lessons about achievements by people of European descent while simultaneously the achievements of Black people are ignored. There were many slaves who participated in escapes, mutinies, and revolts. Any human being forced into slavery would be dissatisfied, hostile, and very angry. From the beginning of America, Black Americans had to fight for freedom and equality. These are true historical facts that should be presented to Americans in order to break down racial barriers. (End of paraphrase).

The following is paraphrased, in part, from a section titled: "Correct Education" by Melvin F. Miller. Dr. Carter G. Woodson was among the first scholars to write about African American history. He devoted his life to the study of his people's history and to their education. He felt that if Blacks did not record their own achievements then other groups would try to falsely claim them as their own.   Dr. Woodson was a child of formerly enslaved African Americans who became -- after the famed scholar W.E.B. Du Bois -- the second Ph.D. graduate of his race from Harvard University. He wrote numerous books about the contributions of Black people to civilization. Arguably, his most well-known work is, "The Mis-Education of the Negro."

Dr. Woodson is most famous for starting a "Negro History Week" observance in 1926 which later became the still observed "Black History Month." In order to build pride and confidence in African heritage, Blacks have to take charge and remove hundreds of years of negative lies and teachings of White superiority over dark-complexioned races. We learned in elementary school about the accomplishments of Christopher Columbus, John Smith, Thomas Edison, Henry Ford, and many other European and American Whites though these teachings were often at the expense of lessons about the many great people of color who achieved remarkable things in American and world history. The knowledge of true African and African American history will enhance one's pride, confidence, love, and respect for one's ancestors and encourage the promotion of the greatness of the African continent. Black Americans survived slavery, segregation, lynching, and brainwashing. All those obstacles were overcome through faith, courage, strength, intelligence, and unity. The persecution of Blacks forced them to unify and resist oppression. In spite of all the injustice and segregation in the United States, Blacks were forced to unify with faith, strength, and courage.

Slavery forced Blacks to feel each other's pain and sorrow with love and understanding among each other. Racist savages, whom Blacks were forced to call their masters, took children from their parents and sold them. This heartbreak was the ultimate of man's inhumanity to man. When that happened to a mother or father all they could ask of the savage, so-called master was whether their child was going to be in a place where there were other Black women? Enslaved women were mothers to all enslaved children, knowing all such children were in desperate need of a mother's love. The loss of a child hurts, but enslaved parents knew they all were forced to expect that could happen to them.

Slavery built a strong unity among Blacks which was also needed after being forced into the new circle of "Jim Crow" segregation. Blacks strived and made progress under segregation. The horrible drawback was injustice, lynching, and other White mob violence. Blacks were forced to live under segregation in a country that brags, "America believes in freedom of choice." Segregation encouraged Blacks to bond together in unity, sisterhood, and brotherhood. Educated and wealthy Blacks had no option to buy homes or estates in rich, elegant neighborhoods -- they had to stay near other Blacks. Educated and rich Blacks were role models in their towns and communities. Black children had many role models to admire, respect, and be encouraged to emulate.

Under segregation, Blacks built great towns and communities in spite of racists' control of capital. Blacks governed their own communities and businesses and owned homes while living in peace and harmony with each other. Whites refused to invest in Black schools, homes, communities, businesses, etc. They permitted money to flow into Black churches in order to have some input and influence. Most great achievements by Blacks have been done on their own with the help and assistance from each other and their communities. Many Blacks displayed love, respect, and admiration for each other in order to survive the terrorist ordeal they lived under in segregated America. Blacks have been great musicians, writers, business people, inventors, educators, spiritual leaders, and politicians fighting for their communities; they have been the envy of racist Whites. Blacks were great songwriters, jazz singers, authors, and inventors of the dance called "The Lindy Hop." Black Americans played an important role in American music and dance. Not only did White

Americans copy their style of music and singing but the whole European continent did as well.

Black love songs were about love and respect for women and men. Racist Whites have also noticed the strength, faith, and courage Blacks gained from segregation. While Blacks were growing in faith, strength, and courage, Whites were chasing fame, fortune, and control over Blacks by any means necessary. Racist Whites enforced segregated laws to keep Whites and Blacks apart from each other and used unjust lynch laws to give it a legal appearance. Racist Whites always misinterpret laws to protect and defend their control over Blacks.

Blacks in America were struggling to survive while White Americans were struggling for fame, fortune, and political power. White Americans set up organized crime, political corruptions, and terrorist KKK organizations to control Black Americans and curtail Black unity and advancement. Blacks could only play servants or stupid comedy roles in U.S. movies while White actors were portrayed as kind and tolerant to Blacks in motion pictures. Blacks were portrayed as stupid, afraid, and unruly people that loved to dance and sing. Whites were portrayed as adventures, lovers, and protectors of Whites from savage Indians or crazy Negroes.

Racist-controlled media portrayed Black men as rapists (of White women), lazy, uneducated, robbers, and irresponsible fools who produced babies and left them fatherless. Racism in America is not any fiction or fantasy but the truth of what America was about during slavery and segregation.

This is a country that preaches freedom and equality for all citizens. It is one thing to talk the talk and another to walk the walk. Equality in America is based on race and color.
 Another influence is how much money you have and to whom you are connected. Greed, power, corruption, and skin color

control this society. Blacks will have to break the control racist Whites have over their lives in order to teach themselves true history and be able to change their own and their children's lives. They need to restore the appreciation for their ancestors who have been lied about in public schools, movies, and the media.

American Blacks must emancipate their minds to become truly free. That will be a tremendous task to overcome after hundreds of years of negative propaganda by a racist-controlled country. To overcome that problem is to first realize and understand the true devastation it caused, and then it will be corrected and defeated by informed and affluent Blacks. Blacks have been fragmented, and this destructive process included controlling their dreams, hopes, and families.

Removing Blacks from their own history, enslaving and brutally exploiting their labor, and limiting and preventing them from building their own future based on the origins of Black civilization, on the very basis of their human rights, were gross and debilitating injustices. American Blacks living under slavery were forcibly conditioned into having their reasoning inverted as perception and reality were mangled and twisted by racism. The horrors and inhumane conditions for Africans on board slave ships is one of man's worst inhumanities to man. These horrors were carried out for centuries and at one time condoned by a U.S. government which proclaimed it had a constitution that promoted freedom and equality for all.

There were differences among Blacks and Whites during the course of history, and feuds and conflicts erupted between them. Blacks were defeated and driven out of Egypt and the surrounding areas. Integration for many hundreds of years between Europeans and Africans has played an important part in changing the complexions of the people of northern Africa and the southern Mediterranean.

During ancient times, Africans were often referred to as Ethiopians and Moors, and Kemet was the ancient name of Egypt. Africa was a continent of Black people who developed great historical and biblical leaders and did not promote racism. They were admired and copied by the world in ancient times. There were great empires in West Africa between 500 and 1600 A.D., including Ghana, Mali, and Songhai. Other major kingdoms on the African continent included the Ashanti Kingdom (1695-1901), and the Kingdom of Cush (1000 B.C.-350 A.D.).

The White race was very eager to remove Blacks' accomplishments, achievements, and spiritual introduction of the Holy Scripture to European culture. They have removed Egypt and countries of the surrounding area out of Africa by labeling them the Middle East. They do not want to refer to those countries as African countries because they know Africa is the Land of the Blacks. Racist Whites portrayed themselves as beautiful people with white skin and straight hair and did not want their people worshiping a spiritual prophet who is Black or has African features. In ancient times, the location where Jesus was born was an area of darker-skinned people. White people are a race in Europe; Black people are a race in Africa. For centuries, Whites have distorted facts about history and religions by leaving the Black race out of history and religions.

King James' Version of the Bible has played a large part in the life of the English-speaking church. There have been many versions of the Bible that have been passed down through history. Most of these versions have been obtained from original scripts that have proof of being originated in Africa. Some European versions of Christianity present Africans' participations in the Holy Bible as that of a race cursed to be servants. That is the reason to know true history and find out true information of the origin of spiritual beliefs and thinking.

African American Historians

African American Historians

This is a list of books written by two well-known African American historians. Just a brief review of the titles of their works will let you know that these authors were concerned with Africa and African American achievements and the uncovering of hidden truths.

Dr. Yosef Ben-Jochannan (also known as "Dr. Ben)":

1. The Need for a Black Bible
2. The Myth of Exodus and Genesis and the Exclusion of Their African Origins
3. Black Man of the Nile and His Family
4. African Origins of Major "Western Religions"
5. We the Black Jews
6. New Dimensions in African History
7. Africa: Mother of Western Civilization
8. A Chronology of the Bible: Challenge to the Standard Version
9. Black Seminarians and Black Clergy without a Black Theology

Dr. John Henrik Clarke:

1. African People in World History
2. Malcolm X: The Man and His Times
3. The Iceman Inheritance: Prehistoric Sources of Western Man's Racism, Sexism and Aggression
4. The Middle Passage: White Ships, Black Cargo
5. Black American Short Stories: A Century of the Best
6. William Styron's Nat Turner: Ten Black Writers Respond
7. Critical Lessons in Slavery & the Slave Trade: Essential Studies & Commentaries on Slavery, in General, & the African Slave Trade, in Particular
8. Harlem Voices from the Soul of Black America

9. Christopher Columbus and the African Holocaust
10. Harlem, U.S.A.
11. New Dimensions in African History
12. Rebellion in Rhyme: the Early Poetry of John Henrik Clarke
13. Africans at the Crossroads: Notes on an African World Revolution
14. My Life in Search of Africa
15. Marcus Garvey and the Vision of Africa

Dr. Yosef Ben-Jochannan specializes in ancient historical eras. Here are descriptions of a few of his books that expose the distortions of history written about Blacks.

1. Black Seminarians and Black Clergy without a Black Theology. With colonization came the dismantling of traditional African belief systems. Influence by the European propaganda mills caused some Africans to believe that they had produced nothing of worth. This is the origin of Black seminarians who could not find a Black Theology. In Black Seminarians, Ben-Jochannan outlines sources of Black Theology before Judaism, Christianity, and Islam. It is important for us to know that the ideas, practices, and concepts that went into the making of Judaism, Christianity, and Islam were already old in Africa before Europe was born. Black Seminarians mark an important first step in our journey to reclaim our spiritual heritage.

2. The Need for a Black Bible. The third book in a three-volume set, The Need for a Black Bible is a companion volume to African Origins of Major "Western Religions" and The Myth of Genesis and Exodus and the Exclusion of Their African Origins. These three volumes were originally published as the three-volume set "The Black Man's Religion," and are available separately for the first time. "The Black Man's Religion" is an invaluable resource for anyone seeking to gain a better understanding of belief systems in the Western World.

3. The Myth of Exodus and Genesis and the Exclusion of Their African Origins. The second in a three-volume set, this is a companion volume to African Origins of the Major "Western Religions" and The Need for a Black Bible.

4. Black Man of the Nile and His Family. First published in 1972. This is Dr. Ben's best-known work. It captures much of the substance of his early research on ancient Africa. In a masterful and unique manner, Dr. Ben uses Black Man of the Nile to challenge and expose "Europeanized" African History. He points up distortion after distortion made in the long record of African contribution to world civilization. He attacks these distortions with a vengeance, providing a spell-binding corrective lesson in our story.

5. A Chronology of the Bible: Challenge to the Standard Version.

First published in 1972 as well, this is another of his most popular works. Originally prepared at the request of a group of Harlem-based ministers, Chronology documents the African origins of Judaism, Christianity, and Islam. Dr. Ben traces significant influences, developments, and people that have shaped and provided the foundation for the holy books used in these religions. I listed these books to inform the public of the roles in history and the Bible in which Africans played a major part. I have used information for the above paragraphs from this web site: http://stewartsynopsis.com/just_bein3.htm

Whites have been superimposed verbally and visually by mass media to give the impression of enormous population compared to Black Americans. Blacks are never mentioned as Americans, they are only mentioned as "Black Americans." American schools teach and preach White history, White heroes, White inventors, and White gods. This is to present White people as the smartest, prettiest, purest, and most innocent people in the world. The media portrays Blacks as crack addicts who live on welfare, indulge in gang warfare, rob, rape, and steal. America has a prison industry which is its fourth largest growing industry. Racist Whites keep it thriving because Blacks are being arrested and locked up in unfair and disproportionate numbers.

Section Two

Highlighting Distortions

Deceptions

and Disunity in America

Distortions

Distortions

One of the main problems in obtaining equality and justice for Black Americans is the continued mind control chains. Humans have concerns to keep their bodies clean, that is why they will bathe frequently. Black Americans have had their minds dirtied for centuries with racist propaganda which states they are not as intelligent, beautiful or civilized as Whites are. It was not only Blacks that were brainwashed to accept this inhuman philosophy; Whites had that preached to them constantly as well. Unfortunately, some Blacks and Whites are stupid or fearful and believe in that propaganda. Blacks must wash their minds from that racist dirt and remove the chains controlling their rights to freedom and equality. When Black Americans accomplish that goal, there will be no power on earth able to denigrate them again. To remove the chains of racist mind control over Blacks, I recommend the study of Black History written by Black historians--and doing research on one's own. Blacks must take control of the education of their children and institute an educational program under their control that will teach their value, culture, and unity, and the greatness of the African continent and its people.

American Jewish citizens have taken charge of their children and taught them their culture, values, etc. They have acquired great strength and influence in America. Catholics have built influential schools and gained political power and influence. The Nation of Islam, under the leadership of Minister Louis Farrakhan, began their educational programs. Their results are obvious when you observe how proud his followers are of their African heritage, their unity and support for each other, and their knowledge of African History.

Those are the elements needed to build a strong, proud race of people. Black people have the money, the brains, and the education to achieve that goal. What is needed is for them to look to themselves and not others to solve their problems. Section one explained some of the racists' tactics used to hinder the unity needed for Blacks to take charge of their own destiny. Blacks have the numbers and the strength to form a rainbow-type coalition party that will include Blacks, Whites, liberals, and all people that believe in equality for all Americans regardless of race or religion, etc. Code words and labels used by the mainstream racists' political parties will not be needed in the Rainbow Coalition Party. When a rainbow-type coalition party is formed that will include people of all colors and races, this will start the beginning of unifying American people. Hopefully, labels like right wing, liberal, non-religious, capitalist, communist, etc. will be used in a descriptive manner and not a derogatory manner. Those labels in this day and time are being used by political parties to degrade people and their party affiliations. If freedom and equality for all Americans is not your belief, you will not be accepted into the rainbow-type coalition party. Believing in equality for all Americans will be the main requirement to become a member of such a party.

This section explains how the media and government control your mind and influence your thoughts and actions: When people understand the ways they are being influenced by a different race other than their own, that is when they will become aware of the mind control problem. With this awareness, Blacks will be energized to work on a solution. The problem they are still facing in this twenty-first century is having their minds controlled by others. Hopefully, this will end and all Americans regardless of race, creed or color will be treated equally. Black communities are neglected by investment banks, state and local governments, under-funded schools, and police who do not look like them and do not live or have an interest in their neighborhoods.

That is a problem Blacks need to take charge of and solve with their God-given faith, strength, courage, and unity.

The following paragraphs contain some unpublicized historical information pertaining to lynching in America. My commentary on the subject of lynching is derived, in part, from information obtained from this web page: http://en.wikipedia.org/wiki/Lynching_in_the_United_States. Any direct quotes entered from this web site will be stated as such. The title is, "Lynching in the United States." Lynching was a program used by racist Whites to keep Blacks and liberal Whites under control. African Americans and White liberals in pursuit of equal rights were frequently lynched in the years following the Reconstruction era and including the Civil Rights era. Southern states created laws between 1890 and 1908 with provisions that effectively disenfranchised most Blacks and many poor Whites. People who were not permitted to vote also were not permitted to serve on juries, further excluding them from the political process.

This era of segregation, lynching, and government conniving in violence against Black Americans forced them to unite to protect themselves. Blacks formed many organizations such as the National Association for the Advancement of Colored People, (NAACP). Numerous groups organized to support this battle for freedom and equality. Black American women were also in the forefront and formed the Association of Southern Women for the prevention of lynching. Their petition drives, letter campaigns, meetings, and demonstrations helped to highlight the issues and combat lynching. In the South, members of the abolitionist movement or other people opposing slavery were often targets of lynch mob violence before the Civil War.

Lynching was prevalent in the southern states as Whites turned to terrorism to prevent Blacks from enjoying freedom and equality. White mob violence was used to prevent Blacks from voting and to enforce Jim Crow laws.

White law enforcement authorities sometimes participated directly in the murderous act of lynching. Sometimes southern police officials held suspects in jails and then allowed mobs to break into these jails so they could abduct and lynch incarcerated Blacks. There is much untold true history of the invasion of Native American territory in the now western United States. What is taught in American schools is the settlement of the West by pioneers and adventurous, law-abiding White people who brought civilization to the Indian savages. American History taught in American schools state that the Indians violated the treaties between them and the White-controlled government of the United States. The Indians are labeled as murderers of peaceful settlers. However, it was the U.S. government which really violated countless treaties and White settlers and soldiers who invaded Native American lands unlawfully and violently.

During American expansion into the western territories of the country, lynching was a part of that movement. Lynching in the new western states involved accused criminals and there were many lynching of Irish, Chinese, and Mexican immigrants. According to historian Michael J. Pfeifer, author of "Rough Justice: Lynching and American Society, 1874-1947," the United States had two systems of "justice," one legal (through the courts) and the other extra-legal (illegal). Both systems "were highly racially polarized, and both operated to enforce White social dominance." (See http://www.greatblacksinwax.org/Exhibits/lynching.htm) White racists in control of state governments passed laws and amendments making voter registration more complicated in order to restrict Black voting rights. State laws created new provisions which included poll taxes, literacy tests, and increased residency requirements that effectively disenfranchised most Blacks and many poor Whites. They forced them off voter registration lists and prevented them from serving on juries.

Although challenges to such laws made their way to the Supreme Court in *Williams v. Mississippi* (1889) and *Giles v. Harris* (1903), the state provisions were upheld.

A direct quote from a paragraph from this web site:
The ideology behind lynching, directly connected with denial of political and social equality, was stated forthright by Benjamin Tillman, then Governor of South Carolina and later a United States Senator: "We of the South have never recognized the right of the Negro to govern white men, and we never will. We have never believed him to be the equal of the white man, and we will not submit to gratifying his lust on our wives and daughters without lynching him." (End of direct quote)

The following paragraph is paraphrased:
The rhetoric surrounding lynching included justifications about protecting White women, however, the basic aim was to maintain White domination in a changing society. (End of paraphrase).

This web site also describes the practice of some people using lynching as a photographic sport. Some even collected lynch souvenirs of murders they had witnessed to send to people. This type of mailing had grown so large in 1908 that the Postmaster General banned the cards from the mail.

The terrorist situation Black Americans faced in America forced them to unite and resist lynching, disenfranchisement, and the loss of their constitutional rights. Hundreds of thousands of Blacks left the South from 1910-1940 to escape lynching and segregation and to seek better lives in industrial cities of the North and Midwest. This resettling was called "The Great Migration." Many secured better education and futures for themselves and their children. They worked on the railroads, in stockyards and meatpacking plants, etc. Racist Whites controlled the southern states and had undue influence over the United States government.

There were too many racist-minded Supreme Court justices appointed to the Supreme Court who ruled against the 14th and 15th Amendments to the Constitution. The crime of lynching in the United States was rarely prosecuted by the people with the authority and responsibility to protect law and order; they were generally in agreement with that criminal act. (End of paraphrase, direct quotes, and comments on some information from this web site).

Black Americans and liberal Whites stood up and protested against the injustice of allowing lynching to happen in the United States. The perpetrators of this injustice were not tried or convicted of committing crimes against Blacks.

In America, the last two verses of the National Anthem are, "In the land of the free" (White people), "and the home of the brave" (Black people). This is my comment on who has been free and who has been brave.

Deception and Disunity in America

Deception and Disunity in America

I will introduce this subject by paraphrasing information on Black American civil rights fighter Paul Robeson. Further information on the life of Paul Robeson can be obtained via the following web pages:
http://en.wikipedia.org/wiki/Paul_Robeson
http://www.africawithin.com/bios/paul_robeson.htm

There were many African American organizations and fighters against American lynching. One of the many great freedom fighters was Paul Robeson. Paul Leroy Robeson was born in Princeton, New Jersey on April 9, 1896. Robeson became a scholar, lawyer, actor, singer, football player, and civil rights advocate. He performed in America and numerous countries around the world. He was one of the world's most celebrated Americans in his lifetime. At the height of his fame, Robeson became a political activist speaking against fascism and racism in the United States and abroad. He spoke against racial segregation and advocated civil rights for all people of color.

Paul Robeson had great friendship with the Soviet Union and its people and believed in its socialism. Robeson worked tirelessly for the liberation of the colonial people of Africa, the Caribbean, and Asia. Included among his efforts were campaigns for anti-lynching legislation, the integration of major league baseball, and many other causes that challenged worldwide White supremacy. Paul Robeson's challenge to international White supremacy caused condemnation from the United States Congress. Under mainstream White control, Congress put him on the anti-American "blacklist" and was able to get predominantly Black organizations, including the NAACP, to withdraw support from Robeson. This degrading act by the American establishment isolated Robeson for the latter part of his career. This persecution virtually erased one of the nation's greatest singers, actors, and humanists from mainstream culture and 20th century history, including civil rights and Black history.

This web site article informs the reader, "To this day, Paul Robeson's FBI file is one of the largest of any entertainer ever investigated by the United States Intelligence Community, requiring its own internal index and unique status of health file." Other sources claim there is documented evidence from the files released under the Freedom of Information Act that Paul Robeson was drugged and neutralized under the CIA's clandestine MKULTRA mind-control program. Robeson was subsequently subjected to unnecessary and abusive levels of electroconvulsive therapy (also known as electroshock treatment) while under private care in Great Britain as a means to keep him from influencing the U.S. civil rights movement and worldwide anti-imperialist movements during the 1960s.

Paul Robeson graduated from Columbia Law School in 1923, and had married Eslanda Cardozo Goode in August 1921. He was the first Black actor in mainstream motion pictures to appear in roles that had dignity and emphasized pride in the African Heritage. Robeson founded the Council on African Affairs (CAA), the first major U.S. organization to focus on providing pertinent and up-to-date information about Africa across the U.S. On January 23, 1976, in Philadelphia, Pennsylvania, he died of a stroke at the age of 78 following complications from a severe cerebral vascular disorder. After his death, Paul Robeson was revered and celebrated throughout the world. Robeson's posthumous tributes and awards from 1976 until the present day number in the thousands. Paul Robeson was a great American and a great citizen of the world who fought for freedom and equality for all humans.

In America, African Americans always had to fight for freedom and equality. In 1951, Black workers formed the National Negro Labor Council (NNLC). This organization was formed to serve the needs and promote the civil rights of Black workers. Some of the founders of the NNLC were, Coleman Young, William Hood, Paul Robeson, Ernest Thompson, and William Marshall. (End of paraphrase).

More information on the NNLC may be found on the following web page:
http://en.wikipedia.org/wiki/National_Negro_Labor_Council
I will paraphrase part of this web page:
The National Negro Labor Council was involved in various important battles to obtain jobs for Blacks and also protested to stop brutal slayings of Blacks by law enforcement. The NNLC carried out many strikes and campaigns to acquire more jobs for African Americans, and fought for their voting rights and equal opportunity to use public facilities as well. Some White union leaders banded together and decided to attack the NNLC. This caused the NNLC to be investigated by the House Un-American Activities Committee which charged them with having communist sympathies. This organization accomplished many tasks relating to civil rights and race discrimination; however, it was forced to come to an end. The NNLC was called before the Subversive Activities Control Board and accused of being a communist front organization. These charges were brought about because the NNLC protested American companies' treatment of Black workers. The legal defense bills to fight these charges were enormous; the NNLC could not afford to pay. The NNLC's leaders voted to dissolve the organization in 1956 because the legal expenses had grown too high for it to survive. (End of paraphrase).

After being freed from the inhumanity of slavery, Black Americans faced brutal racism, lynching, and segregation. These uncivilized conditions forced Blacks to unite and resist United States oppression against them. Freedom was felt by

Blacks only in their neighborhoods and communities. Whites and Blacks were prohibited from integrating with each other under some state laws and real estate restrictions. This spawned a new movement with Blacks to become independent from Whites. This movement encouraged Black culture and intellectual life. This was a movement that impacted many urban centers and towns in the United States where Blacks created their own literature, music, art, dance, and entertainment. Black America's mind was becoming focused on Black ideology, goals, virtues, and creativity.

Black Americans, after hundreds of years of White racist brainwashing, began to reject the practice of imitating the styles of Europeans and American Whites. They began to accept their true selves, and created their own Black culture. They also accepted their true identity and their cultural ties to Mother Africa. This independent Black movement was a strong achievement for their culture and played a major part in attracting White Americans' attention. Whites labeled this movement "The Harlem Renaissance," because the Black community in Harlem played such an important role in building and presenting the greatness of Black Americans. This movement was also known as the Black Literary Renaissance and the New Negro Movement. This movement highlighted the greatness of African American literature, drama, music, visual arts, sociology, and history, and exposed many of the problems facing Black Americans.

During the past, Whites designated Black Americans as the Negro race. Negro is not a race; it is just a Spanish word for "black." Hundreds of years of White brainwashing have caused African Americans to accept that "Negro" label.
The civil rights movements have discarded that "Negro" label and American Blacks returned to their racial identity as a proud Black Race from Africa.

Racist Whites kept a jealous eye on the Harlem Renaissance movement. This movement enabled many African Americans to attain middle class status. Blacks organized themselves politically and intellectually. Whites were becoming increasingly fascinated by Black culture. The more Blacks progressed in spite of segregation, lynching, and racism, Whites in power used this as a means to proclaim equality and freedom in America. Whites will display the best White neighborhoods to be compared to the worst Black neighborhoods. They also would refer to White America and Black America as separate and unequal. African Americans banded together and supported a number of political movements which helped them in their goal for freedom and equality. During American segregation, there were many conflicts of economic competition over jobs, housing, and social territories. These conditions contributed to racist mob violence that forced Blacks to organize and become politically active. Segregation in America led Blacks to a stronger social consciousness. Their many great inventions, music, dance, entertainment, writings, creating blood plasma transfusions, and being the first to perform a heart operation, etc., placed Black Americans on the world stage, providing them with international contacts. American Blacks had to re-educate themselves from hundreds of years of brainwashing, distortions of history and lies. Black historians have searched back into ancient times and exposed European lies against Africa and the Black race and culture.

Black music during segregation was about love, strength, faith, courage, hope, and triumph. At that time, they did not sing songs that disgraced Black women or men. The "N word" or "B word" was not used in songs or comedy entertainment. During segregation, Blacks respected themselves more and felt each other's pain. In spite of segregation, lynching, and lynch laws, they controlled their own social circles and beliefs. Forced segregation permitted Blacks to be themselves and bond with each other. Blacks built great towns, communities, and houses of worship, formed their own baseball leagues and beauty pageants, produced their own movies, and appeared in such world famous places of entertainment as the Apollo Theater, Savoy Ballroom, Renaissance Ballroom, and Small's Paradise where only the best in Black entertainment was the rule.

The following is a list of just some of the many outstanding individuals from the Harlem Renaissance period and immediately after. Many more could be added.

Novelists: Jessie Redmon Fauset -- (There is Confusion) (1924); Rudolf Fisher -- (The Walls of Jericho) (1928); Langston Hughes -- (Not Without Laughter) (1930).

Actors and Dramatists: Paul Robeson (Actor); Langston Hughes ("Mulatto," an opera); Zora Neale Hurston ("Color Struck.").

Poets: Langston Hughes (poet, fiction writer, essayist, etc.); Jessie Redmon Fauset (editor, poet, essayist, and novelist); Countee Cullen (poet and novelist); Claude McKay (poet and novelist); May Miller (poet and playwright); Alice Dunbar-Nelson (poet and fiction writer).

Leading Intellectuals: W.E.B. Du Bois; Alain Locke; Walter White; Mary White Ovington; A. Philip Randolph; Marcus Garvey; Arthur Schomburg.

Visual Artists: Jacob Lawrence; Charles Alston; Henry W. Bannarn; Aaron Douglas; Lois Mailou Jones.

Musicians, Composers, Entertainers: Billie Holiday; Duke Ellington; Count Basie; Louis Armstrong; Coleman Hawkins; Sidney Bechet; Eubie Blake; Bessie Smith; Fats Waller; Noble Sissle; Earl "Fatha" Hines; Jelly Roll Morton; Josephine Baker; Lena Horne; Ella Fitzgerald; Bill "Bojangles" Robinson; The Nicholas Brothers; Marian Anderson; Ethel Waters; Moms Mabley; The Will Mastin Trio; Cab Calloway; The Nat King Cole Trio; Chick Webb; Lionel Hampton; Mary Lou Williams; Nipsey Russell; Roy Hamilton.

Whenever, and if ever, the truth of the holocaust of slavery, lynching, segregation, injustice, and lies about Ancient History and American History is revealed, that will be the day to marvel at the horrors Blacks have overcome. Black historians, educators, and civil rights activists rescued African Americans from returning to the ignorance of White supremacy and its values. In America, citizens are taught that the Constitution represents freedom and equality for all Americans. America proclaims to be the best democratic country in the world. (Your words will introduce who you are. Your actions will prove who you are).

The achievements of Black Americans during segregation impressed many Americans of all backgrounds. Southern states enforced strict segregation to keep Whites and Blacks apart. Blacks were permitted a certain degree of integration in the North. Northern states discouraged integrated neighborhoods, however, yet, Whites attended many Black night clubs, ballrooms, and other places of entertainment. While many entertainment activities in the North were integrated, Black entertainment activities attended by both races in the South were separated by a rope; Whites were on one side and Blacks were on the other side, and this was enforced by police officers.

Unjust conditions forced Blacks and liberal Whites to unite and challenge them. The Black civil rights movement gained strength and momentum. That movement started with the determination to obtain freedom and equality. The racist White media redefined that movement from one seeking freedom and equality to seeking "integration." However, winning a fight for freedom and equality will automatically guarantee integration.

The racist media have a way of mitigating or controlling the grievances or themes of African American complaints. During the era of segregation, the media admitted there were two Americas that were separate and unequal. The media, politicians, and government officials constantly referred to America as a free and equal society. The media constantly highlighted crime, drugs, shanty homes, and any negative event in Black areas.

Reporting by the media about White areas was always positive compared to the negative reporting about Black neighborhoods.

In White areas there were so-called organized crimes, also drug crimes, corruptions by politicians and law enforcement officials. Crimes are committed by people of all races. No one race has a monopoly on crime. The media will expose criminal activity by Whites as a rare occasion. Black criminal deeds are presented as a constant event. The media is biased in favorable reporting concerning White-on-White crime compared to unfavorable reporting about crimes committed by Blacks against each other.

Greedy legislators or public officials will accept bribes from businesses or corporations for agreeing to pass their votes for or against any legislation, they desire. These politicians have control of the law and the wording of legal interpretations. Bribery is an obvious crime; in order to avoid being charged with bribery, greedy officials state that receiving gifts or money is a normal lobbying procedure. They claim money and gifts received from lobbyists are donations to their political campaign to help in their re-election. Greedy politicians have changed the word bribery to "lobbying," giving that word a legitimate meaning.

Black Americans were brainwashed to believe in White gods, that White is beautiful and Black is ugly. This propaganda repeated during 400 years of brainwashing has taken its toll on all Americans to this very day. These are just words to present a feeling either of praise or of ridicule, to make a person feel proud and good or make them feel bad or ashamed of themselves. America, during the era of slavery, segregation, and unequal law enforcement, continued to keep Americans divided against each other. It was the civil rights rebellion's unity of Black Americans and Liberal Whites protesting together against injustice that changed things for the better. The fight for equality and justice is not over; there are still too many right-wing racists and Negroes to overcome before America will be a united country.

A united country is a country where citizens are judged by the content of their character and not by the color of their skin, their religion, or how many millions of dollars they own. (Your words will introduce who you are; your actions will prove who you are).

Some religious organizations will denounce abortion as a moral sin. All through the history of slavery, lynching, and racism, there has never been a countrywide cry in America from religious organizations against the immoral sin of slavery. Slavery was not preached against in most White churches. There were certain churches and religious officials that preached against slavery, but they were ridiculed and persecuted by racist politicians in control.

The following information is paraphrased from this web site: http://www.okcjournal.com/ministry-greed.htm
The title is: "Are Some Preachers Overdosing on Greed?"
By Rev. Dr. Barbara Reynolds.
There are fighters in America for justice and equality and there are those who fight for greed and selfishness. Greed and selfishness knows no religion, race, or politics, etc. Unfortunately, greed has taken control of American society. It is also infested in some churches and religions. Ministers of very large churches with large congregations will not preach about the damnation of greed and the love of money as being the root of all evil. Times have changed from the earlier days where ministers once preached the lesson that Christians should do for others before they do for themselves.

Many spiritual leaders of this era are busy writing books and promoting their CDs on the subject of religion to promote sales from believers. They do not preach against greed and abusers of the poor and needy as they did in sermons of the past. Sermons of today seem to be encouraging accumulating wealth and prosperity for self; being aware of people and not of your faith. Some spiritual leaders rather sell their books and own expensive cars than organize a congregation and help the needy to improve. Ministers today can be helpful to mobilize against crime and help people recently released from jails to improve their lives. Some seem to support materialism as more important than servant-hood and the goal of salvation which will require sacrifice. The working poor and the needy are being plundered and many preachers have little to say about it. (End of paraphrase).

Today, there are many mega-church ministers of different races writing books and producing CDs. Some ministers are more devoted to succeeding as religious pimps than to leading as Jesus Christ did to work for human rights, equality, and a happy, inspirational, full life. Black preachers have not ridiculed the institution of slavery in America and demanded a confession of the committed sin of slavery by this government. Slavery is against the life and teachings of Jesus Christ and that can be proven by reading the Bible. These preachers need to be more concerned about uplifting communities than promoting their books or CDs. They also should follow the examples of Jesus Christ's teachings and leadership.

Blacks, with the help of liberal Whites, resisted racism and segregation and finally started to win legal court battles in the Supreme Court outlawing racism and segregation.
Those victories curtailed White control over Black Americans. Racist Whites were determined to keep control by permitting drugs in Black neighborhoods and using lynch-law tactics in our so-called legal system to convict Blacks and lock them into prisons. Some examples of lynch-law tactics are as follows: Drug laws are set-up to separate certain drugs used mostly by Whites from drugs used mostly by Blacks. For example, powder cocaine is claimed as White used and crack cocaine is claimed as Black used. The law is written so crack cocaine possession is a more serious crime with longer jail time as punishment. Blacks who are sent to prison serve their time and, when released, often

lose their right to vote. Blacks are released back into society with prison records and therefore unable to get employment.
Blacks faced with criminal charges have to face a racist judicial system, racist district attorneys, and sometimes questionable, so-called scientific evidence. When two or more Blacks are arrested, the district attorney works deals to have one defendant turn against the other. Regardless of the seriousness of the crime, or who actually committed the more violent act, one defendant only has to agree to testify as the prosecutor advised him. When a defendant agrees to cooperate with the prosecutors, he receives a suspended sentence or minor charge violation. Sometimes an innocent Black is convicted by a so-called informer with a criminal record in order to reduce his criminal charges. He will agree to any prosecutor's offer of leniency and sometimes say anything he is told to say.

Information pertaining to this police action was obtained from this web site: www.cathyharrisspeaks.com. Updated information on criminal charges was posted on this web site: www.justice4ericjohnson.com, at the time of this action.
This police action involves Eric A. Johnson who recently graduated from Creeside High School in Georgia as an honor student and member of the Beta Club. He has been working months to help support his mother and had planned to attend Westwood College in January 2010. Eric lost his father in a tragic house fire accident. Eric has faced adversity and overcome numerous obstacles to become a successful young man.

Information from the web site is paraphrased by me as follows: On Monday night, August 17, 2009, Antoine Wimes and Donavan McCoy were charged with shooting Nikki Neely and afflicting serious injury to her 10-month-old baby in a vicious and senseless home invasion. On August 18, 2009, Eric saw the news report on this horrific attack, called 911, and reported to police that he had given a ride to the suspects earlier in the evening. Eric gave his statement to Officer Byars of the Fulton County Police Department. Eric told Officer Byars he was asked

115

by Antoine Wimes to give him a ride in exchange for gas money. Eric picked up Antoine Wimes and another young man that he met for the first time named "Dino." He drove them to the gas station, bought gas, took them further down South Fulton Parkway, and dropped them off. The police obtained and reviewed the gas station video that confirms Eric was at the gas station at 5:45 p.m.

Donavan McCoy's initial statement to police was that he and Antoine Wimes were dropped off. Another independent witness, Virginia Bonylan, reported to police that she saw Antoine Wimes and Donavan McCoy in the area at 7:30 p.m. She did not see or identify Eric Johnson as being with Antoine Wimes or Donavan McCoy. During the hearing, Ms. Bonylan testified that Antoine Wimes and Donavan McCoy were coming out of Johnny Jones' driveway when she saw them. Ms. Bonylan saw these two men again later, at 10:30 p.m., and gave them a ride.

A statement from this site states: "We have an alibi witness that Eric Johnson was home well before dark on August 17, 2009." On August 17, 2009, Eric told Officer Byars he knew Antoine Wimes when living in the same subdivision previously. Officer Byars informed Eric and his mother, Loleta Horton, the Chattahoochee Hills Police would contact them. Eric claims he had a conversation with the Chattahoochee Hills police detectives without the presence of an attorney. On Thursday, August 27, 2009, Eric was arrested at his home in Union City.

During the Bond Hearing, the lead detective, Jamie Melton, admitted that he had no evidence that Eric A. Johnson was present at the time of the shooting or knew that Antoine Wimes and Donavan McCoy intended to commit any crime. The detective additionally testified under oath that if Eric A. Johnson had talked to him he would not have obtained an arrest warrant. Eric Johnson is charged with multiple felonies including: two counts of Aggravated Battery, Armed Robbery, and Aggravated Assault with a deadly weapon, and Cruelty to Children. Judge

Goger granted a total bond of $50,000. Eric remains in jail unable to post bond, his mother is unemployed and his father is deceased. Reverend Derrick Rice, M. Div., Pastor of Sankofa United Church of Christ, is instrumental in seeking justice for Eric Johnson with the involvement of many others. (End of paraphrase).

I write this book in honor and respect of my ancestors and the Black race. All through American History, Blacks have been ridiculed, dehumanized, and persecuted. I am determined to present the truth, and honor the African American citizens that have tried with the help of liberal Whites to make America a great country that truly believes in equality and justice for all.

A man named Donald Eugene Gates, now age 58, spent 28 years in jail for being convicted of rape and murder. He was cleared and released from jail after DNA showed he was innocent. He had been convicted largely because of the testimony of an FBI forensic analyst whose work later came under fire and whose hair analysis technique has been discredited. Gates had been convicted in 1961 for the rape and murder of Catherine Schilling which took place in Washington, D.C.'s Rock Creek Park. She was a 21-year-old Georgetown University student. His sentence was 20 years to life. There have been times when FBI crime labs have been suspected of siding with the prosecution.

Barry Scheck, co-director of the Innocence Project, has said judges as well as prosecutors need to be informed when crime lab analyses are called into question.

The 2008 presidential election proved the majority of Americans wanted a change from racism, government greed, selfishness, political divisions, and corruption. They elected a candidate that promoted their desire for America to be taken in a new direction from the past failed policies. This newly-elected United States president had the look and features of an African. His name is

Barack Hussein Obama. President Obama is bi-racial. He had a White mother and an African father. He has made it known his presidency is not about a Black man or a White man, but about the welfare and greatness for all. He is the President for America, for its entire people. It was the majority White population that made the 2008 Presidential election a realization of Dr. Martin Luther King's dreams. The majority of the white voting population proved its greatness and belief in the equality for all Americans.

Many American Whites and Blacks are of mixed blood. However, there are still many racist politicians and racist media trying to keep Americans divided.

President Obama and his beautiful wife, First Lady Michelle Obama, are examples for all Americans to be inspired by the role model of family values. The media has deliberately distorted Black family values. President Obama and First Lady Michelle have refuted the media's lies and distortions about Black family values. First Lady Michelle Obama's parents are also family role models do to the great achievements they have made while living under segregation and racism. The media portrays White family values as virtuous and highly regarded. They also portray Black family values in negative reporting and constantly state facts about fatherless Black families. Comparing the reported amount of the Black population in America to the reported amount of Whites, these numbers alone are proof there are more White fatherless homes in America. White men commit crimes, look for sex, and tell lies, cheat, and steal just as men of other races are capable of doing. The media treats fatherless homes in America as a Black problem and not an American problem. That alone proves biased reporting.

To this very day, racist Whites will do whatever they can to discredit Blacks, and dehumanize or make them fail. Not all law officers are racist. There have been incidents of racist officers hired. They have caused confusion, murder, disunity, and instigated crime problems in Black areas. The national media deliberately reports crimes happening in cities that have Black mayors. Their intentions are to influence the public that Black mayors are not as able to govern as effectively as White mayors. This is another problem that needs careful scrutiny and the need for community vigilance and observation. A Black elected mayor or governor of a city or state with a very large Black population will be blamed for a rise in crime, drug trafficking, and youth mob violence plus anything negative to discredit confidence in Blacks running a stable office. Whenever a White male is elected to the same town or state a Black official was at one time in control of, the media will not say that the White official solved Black crime problems. Under White control, the media will report a drop in crime. The media will continue to report and highlight numerous crimes committed in Black neighborhoods regardless of whether a Black or White mayor or governor is in control. A Black official will be exposed as unable to solve crimes or other problems, etc.

In the year 2008, Liberal Whites and African Americans united to elect Illinois Senator Barack Obama as President of the United States. He became president when the American economy was on the verge of collapse. This collapse was in progress for many years under the rule of injustice, discrimination, greed, and corruption. White rule controlled inequality between the haves and have-nots and promoted the influence of special interests in political parties instead of equality and equal opportunity for all Americans. President Obama's election was encouraged by his promise to change America from a land of political greed and advantages, remove corruption, and be more concerned for the welfare of the citizens and not a political party. Many Americans were inspired by him with his message of hope and the wish for a change to a better America for all. They finally wanted America to walk the walk it preached and talked about for hundreds of years. During the 2008 elections, many Whites proved they wanted to live in peace and harmony with their fellow Americans of all races.

In three years of his leadership, President Obama has accomplished a great deal since he took office in January 2009. He has passed comprehensive health care reform legislation with the help of Congress and in spite of intense resistance from the Republican Party. Other accomplishments include, pulling our economy back from the brink of collapse, better regulating our financial and investment markets, securing additional relief for those who are unemployed, ending the war in Iraq, and improving America's stature in the world community. The majority of American White and Black voters wanted to elect a Black president in 2008, but this did not end racism in America. Many Americans, including President Obama, are aware racism still exists in America. Racism has existed in America hundreds of years, and that condition could not disappear suddenly because of an election. In fact, a racist climate has been fostered in the media by certain pundits and racist politicians in order to keep the country divided.

The mainstream media publicize so-called political groups that criticize President Obama and encourage that type of critics with the statement; "this is America with free speech." Media will not discourage critics from telling lies. They give the impression of encouraging lies and disputes. As President Obama and his family occupy the "White House," he performs his presidential duties with more sincerity and conviction than any president before him did. Presidents before Obama did not have to solve the enormous problems he inherited from President George W. Bush. Presidents before President Obama never received the scrutiny which he has encountered. The media portrays President Obama as "Damned if he does and damned if he does not."

Whatever President Obama does, the media publishes articles criticizing him with statements such as, "Why is he doing this or that?" "Why is he not doing this or that?" The media will not side with him and state, "He is the President of the United States and must address all problems pertaining to the welfare of America." Barack Obama is a president that does not pick or choose what problem needs to be solved. He believes all problems need to be taken care of, and he has appointed cabinet members and knowledgeable people in charge to help fix problems his presidency has inherited. The media use any statement President Obama says and interpret it in a manner that deliberately challenges him and causes controversies. They will mention news activities and use those events to report biased information for or against the concerned subjects. The media is more interested in making news instead of reporting fair and balanced news.

President Obama has faced major challenges during his first term of presidency. The Republican Party and segregationists are doing everything to block his initiatives and request for all parties to work together to improve the economy and increase jobs, etc., for all Americans. President Obama understands the problems and has the common sense not to let biased media or racists dictate his actions, programs, or presidency. (With that knowledge and understanding, his hair has become a little gray but not all gray).

President Obama has the ability to remain calm above this fracas and display his optimism and faith in the American people. I know he will continue his term displaying his human qualities with intelligence and determination to improve America for all Americans and show the world America believes in cooperation and peace with other countries. His goal is to bring peace, economic stability, equality, and great opportunity for Americans to live with prosperity. He also understands that to succeed in his wish for a better America, help is needed from the American people. Fortunately, his presidency has forced racists to expose themselves in the fight against unity, equality, and justice for all. Racists will do all they can to not let a Black president succeed in office. President Barack Obama, in being classified as the first Black president, is held to a higher standard than any White president before him. All of the White presidents were treated with the greatest respect deserving of the president of the United States. Racists have disrespected him and constantly refer to him by using only his last name instead of a more respectful address such as "Mr. President" or "Mr. Obama" or "President Obama."

Regardless of how decent, patriotic, or intelligent he is or how concerned he is for all citizens, the fact that he is Black means that they do not want the first Black President to be labeled as a success historically. They do not want him to continue to make history and be re-elected for a second term. Racist Whites realize he would set progressive, beneficial goals that would be impossible for them to deny without incurring the wrath of the American people. President Obama's intelligence and great knowledge is so overwhelming to prejudiced people that they try to counteract it with the sentiment, "He uses arrogance in his talking points and tries to influence people to accept him as a political rock star." In other words, he is being "uppity" and is all charisma without substance; sometimes one has to translate what is expressed to get at the truth of what biased people are saying.

The media conducts polls to convince the public that President Obama is not connecting with American citizens. They accuse him of confusing the issues, not addressing important issues quickly, and not displaying enough anger or being too cool and calm when people are suffering, etc. They claim his approval ratings are low. The media highlights his problems and not his successes. They do not focus on the negative acts of politicians who block his programs for improving the economy, increasing jobs, rebuilding America's infrastructure, etc. This is a program to discourage Americans from re-electing the first Black President. When the media proclaims his approval ratings are dropping to a low point, be careful and observant of a corrupt re-election. The media has started early in President Obama's term by stating what he has not accomplished instead of stating what he has accomplished. This is proof of the determination to encourage the public to not re-elect him.

This country has racist logos. America is a multi-racial country that represents many colors. Therefore, the White House should not be painted to represent only the White race. It should be painted in a diversity of colors to remove White-only logos and signs. Unfortunately, the only predominant color is white which represents White control. To keep the President's house painted white is a message from racists. The President's house needs to be referred to as the People's House and not the White House. The People's House needs to represent all races and not just the White race. When that happens, there will be unity and progress to mitigate racist control.

Great human rights leaders of the past are: Mahatma Gandhi of India, he freed India from British control, and he was assassinated. Dr. Martin Luther King, Jr. of America brought Whites and Blacks together to fight for equality and freedom. Dr. King was assassinated. President Abraham Lincoln freed Black Americans from slavery. He was assassinated. President Franklin D. Roosevelt saved the country from economic destruction. In the year 1940, President Roosevelt issued an executive order establishing the Fair Employment Practices Commission, forbidding discrimination in government and defense industries. He died of natural causes. His presidency was helped by his wife, First Lady Eleanor Roosevelt, who tried to break down racial barriers in America. President Jimmy Carter was not afraid to challenge racist agendas and statements. President Bill Clinton appointed Blacks to his cabinet in important positions and promoted racial tolerance. There are many great fighters in America and in African countries that are determined to fight for equality and fair justice; they are too many to name and not all may be recognized. I hope this book will encourage tolerance, and that the readers will not accept information solely on what is read or heard. I hope you will be encouraged to double-check all information before making a judgment. The Internet can also be used to check information on various subjects pertaining to history and politics.

Another great African American freedom fighter is Harry Belafonte who is known all over the world for his courage to fight for freedom and equality. Belafonte is an important activist of African American history. (Your words will introduce who you are; your actions will prove who you are).

There are some politicians in government that have important governing roles and will try to change laws to their political advantage and assure that their party will be reelected. They will use so-call legal reasons to remove citizens' rights to vote. Taking away your right to vote is effectively taking away your citizenship. That action will encourage non-voters to remove their dedication and obligations in supporting rules that keep them from participating in a so-called free and equal society.

Information used in this book was obtained from the historians, the internet, scholars, media, also my scholastic education, and observations.

Summary

Summary

Black Americans have removed the chains from their wrists and ankles, and also stopped savages from lynching them by the neck on tree branches. Now is the time for American Blacks to remove the chains from their minds by educating themselves about their heritage of African achievement and the greatness of the African race. Blacks have been brainwashed about European history through lies and distortions. The moment to learn the truth about the greatness of the Black race is way past due.

American Blacks should never make the statement, "Our ancestors were born slaves." Human beings are not born slaves, some are, unfortunately, born into an inhumane society that supports and condones the savagery of slavery. The Creator of humanity does not create slaves. Slavery is an unjust condition created by savages in order to subdue people whom they feared and/or desired to exploit their physical and intellectual resources after kidnapping and defeating them in combat. When you make the statement, "my ancestors were born slaves," you do not realize that statement is technically blaming God for creating slaves and not blaming the inhumanity on humans.

To remove a chain from your brain, you have to know what the key is. Black and White Americans have to realize the key is obtaining the truth behind the distortions of European and American history, including the lies about African and Native American (Indian) culture. These lies and distortions are still taught in schools and broadcast by the media in a way that is more subtle than the method used when I was growing up. We have to recognize that the role of the media is to influence the population and guide their actions in the direction it wants.

The media also instigates conflicts between groups and organizations in order to promote confusion and even the termination of particular civil rights organizations. The basic responsibility of African American survival under American segregation was to take control of their world and create the unity, comfort, and pleasure that made their communities strong.

The media displayed Black towns and communities as degraded slums and run-down homes. The era of segregation forced Blacks to unify and support their communities and raise themselves to be dignified and purposeful. Segregation was the era when Blacks built prosperous towns and neighborhoods, including the Greenwood district in Tulsa, Oklahoma that was known as the Black Wall Street. That town was destroyed and Black residents were murdered by envious White Racists.

Blacks proved they are capable of surviving on their own; they have created their own businesses, Black beauty contests, baseball leagues, movies, music industries, newspapers, great poetry writers, songwriters, inventors, etc. I could continue on and on about Black independence and achievements. The more Blacks achieved on their own without White support, the more Whites became envious and jealous. They used the media to promote White supremacy and their achievements. The media promoted this while downgrading the achievements of Blacks and other people of color; the same lies and distortions about Blacks and Native Americans continue in American popular culture and are being spread with better technology.

The media does not promote unity or cooperation; it promotes divisions and fear, using conflict as an opportunity to influence and control events and outcomes. The media is owned by corporations and the wealthy that exert great influence over government officials and the politics of America. The birth of America was about preserving both the enslavement of Blacks and White control. Owners of slaves were among those who wrote the original United States Constitution.

White men took advantage of Black women during slavery, forcing them to have sex. Their children were born into slavery with the indefensible consent of their White fathers. This is the main reason why America is a mixed race nation. Most racist Whites will deny America is a mixed race nation. However, many mixed race Blacks were able to pass as White people, thinking that it was the only way to escape inhumane treatment under forced slavery and other racist practices in the United States.

America is a country filled with many people of mixed race background. Today, with the integration of many nations, we are practically living in a mixed race world. Unfortunately, America still has racists in positions of power who continue to influence policy while spreading lies, fear, and disunity in America. During the time of the recent census, I came to the conclusion that counting the U.S. population every ten years is racially inaccurate because mixed race people will sometimes choose to be counted as members of the White race in order to claim the advantages White people have in a racist society. The 2010 census form, when asking for race determination, actually had the word "Negro" as a possible selection. However, Negro is not a race; it is a Spanish word for the color black.

Undercounting the Black population is a major hindrance to Black representation in this democracy. In addition, gerrymandering is a significant factor in keeping the Black population under White control as it gives the majority population the power to keep electing their own and stop Blacks (and other non-Whites) from becoming a majority that would have more votes in a particular district. With gerrymandering in effect, can Blacks elect candidates of their choice? Black American citizens and politicians should demand that the actions of slavery, lynching, and unequal laws enforced in this society during American History be acknowledged. The reason for that statement is because some of those conditions exist today.

America still has a long way to travel to right all the wrongs it has committed against people of color. It is true that there have been many great improvements since the end of the Civil Rights Era, and the 2008 presidential election has proven that there are many Whites who are not racist. While the media continues to try to divide Americans by race, political party, class, etc., it is hoped by this author that his small book will help spread the word that knowledge is power and the truth does set you free.

My first book was about African Americans removing chains from their ankles and wrists, and surviving slavery, segregation, lynching, and injustices. This book is about African Americans removing the chains from their minds and taking control of their lives and their children's lives and learning true African history and American history.

Politicians campaigning to be elected to office will claim they believe in and support the United States Constitution. That is their right but it is important for Americans and especially African Americans to be sure which Constitution they are referring to. There are two versions of the Constitution. The first version included the words of slave owners supporting and condoning slavery. The second version was changed by adding the 13th, 14th, and 15th Amendments after the Civil War that ended slavery and guaranteed freedom, equality, and voting rights to Blacks. It is thus very important for voters to be sure which Constitution a politician is in support of, the one before the Civil War or the one after the Civil War. This is information that should be acknowledged and discussed. I make that statement because it is important to know exactly where political office seekers stand and what their beliefs truly are.

My two books explain how low a race will go in order to promote themselves as the best. Example: To put and keep a race in a ditch of fear, untruth, mistrust, and confusion forces a race to become the one they want to defame.

Promoting lies and distortions, etc. of Blacks is a cover-up for the inhumane treatment and mis-education not only of Blacks but of Whites as well.

This book is written to present situations that have happened and to display reasons for taking control of your own life by making it your responsibility to take charge of educating your race about the greatness and accomplishments of your people and ancestors.

Pick up the keys and learn the truth of African History and American History. I hope the readers of this book will find it to be very informative.

The author hopes the division of beliefs and religions will dissolve among humans as we become more understanding of each other's historical experience. Humans are an integrated and mixed race of people. It is time to bring love, respect, cooperation, assistance, and equality on Earth. We need to remove from Earth the Devil of hell, greed, and the selfishness of power and control by a certain few; we must remove inequality. An example of inequality: One obvious method being used is the voting suppression of the 2012 presidential election trying to defeat the first black president of the United States from being reelected.

Blacks should be prepared to protect themselves by organizing their agendas to set-up true African History, etc. Select the knowledgeable historians. Be prepared to unite and stand against negative statements from the media and commentators.

Dr.Martin Luther King, Jr. had a dream for racial equality and equal justice for all Americans. He worked hard and forceful for his dream to come true. He made great accomplishments to fulfill his goal, but there is still more hard work to be done.

The goal of this book is to present a new proud understanding of how our ancestors endured slavery, savagery, and hate in the United States. Knowing the past is the tool that will prepare and unite a people in gaining the strength and knowledge to know how they could preserve and protect themselves in the future. When you know true history, you will realize Africans have been the envy of the world.

Books with important African American Historical information:

1. African American Lives: Edited by, Henry Louis Gates Jr. and Evelyn Brooks Higginbotham

2. African American Desk Reference: Schomburg Center for research in Black Culture. The Ultimate Source for Essential information about History, Culture, and Contemporary Life